Man-Made Monsters

Man-Made Monsters

A Field Guide to Golems, Patchwork Soldiers, Homunculi, and Other Created Creatures

By Dr. Bob Curran

Illustrated by Ian Daniels

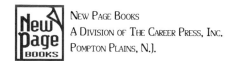

New Page Books
A Division of The Career Press, Inc.
Pompton Plains, N.J.

MAN-MADE MONSTERS
EDITED AND TYPESET BY GINA TALUCCI HOOGERHYDE
Cover art and interior illustrations by Ian Daniels
Printed in the U.S.A. by Imperial Impressions

To order this title, please call toll-free 1-800-CAREER-1 (NJ and Canada: 201-848-0310) to order using VISA or MasterCard, or for further information on books from Career Press.

The Career Press, Inc.
220 West Parkway, Unit 12
Pompton Plains, NJ 07444
www.careerpress.com
www.newpagebooks.com

Library of Congress Cataloging-in-Publication Data

Curran, Bob.
    Man-made monsters : a field guide to golems, patchwork soldiers,
    homunculi, and other created creatures / by Bob Curran.
         p. cm.
Includes index.
ISBN 978-1-60163-136-7 -- ISBN 978-1-60163-707-9 (ebook)
    1. Monsters--Folklore. 2. Animals, Mythical. 3. Artificial life. I. Title.

GR825.C87 2011
001.944--dc22

                                                                2010025414

CONTENTS

Introduction

Children
of
Clay

...LIKE A GREAT SHADOW OR SCARECROWE, THE SEMBLANCE OF A MAN...

—LAWRENCE CLARKSON, *THE RIGHT DEVIL DISCOVER'D*

ONE MORNING IN THE 1730s, a young man stood in front of a cabinet in the offices of the Burgomeister of Hamburg, which contained a fearful and legendary creature. The young man's name was Carl Linnaeus; he would later go on to become one of the leading naturalists of his day, second only to Charles Darwin. The creature at which he stared was said to be the terrible Hydra of Greek fable and myth. It had allegedly been caught and killed several centuries earlier, its remains taken as part of plunder after the looting of Prague in 1648, and it had eventually become the property of the Count of Konigsmark. Later on, it became the possession of the Burgomeister of Hamburg, who had written to Linnaeus at his home in Sweden asking him to come and inspect it.

The creature was truly an awesome and frightening specimen. It had seven heads, sharp teeth, claws, and a snake-like body. It had been the subject of much scientific enquiry and had been included in a number of naturalistic compendia as a creature from a bygone age or some sort of monster left over from the formation of the world. The Hydra of Hamburg was one of a number of monsters held by the nobility of Europe at the time, which hinted at strange and frightening times when such things had actually roamed the Earth and had also become tinged with supernatural elements.

When Linnaeus arrived in Hamburg, the Burgomeister was engaged in selling the specimen for a rather substantial profit. One of the prospective buyers was even the King of Denmark. Indeed, the reason for the natural-ist's visit was to authenticate the monster as a bone fide animal in order to increase its commercial value. However, as he examined it closely, Linneaus discovered something startling: the monster had been made by men, and it had been cobbled together from a number of sources. The claws, for example, were actually the feet of extremely large weasels; the serpent-like "hide" of the monster was in fact the skins of several varieties of snake, all carefully grafted together, and the skeleton comprised the bones of a number of large mammals. A skilled taxidermist had also been employed in its construction. Nevertheless, this bizarre forgery showed signs of great antiquity and, in Linnaeus's view, it had not been put together to dupe the potential clients who were thinking of buying it. His belief was that it had been a construct, prepared by early Christian monks in order to terrify the faithful into believing that the end of the world was at hand. The "Hydra," he believed, was portrayed as a creature from the book of Revelations designed to keep wayward persons from wandering, and to assure them of the truth of the Christian Gospel. Perhaps the monks had even created some semblance of movement in it to add additional terror to its appearance. It was, in every sense, a man-made monster.

Origins of the Monster

The word *monster* has two possible origins, both from Latin. The first is *monstrum* meaning "an omen," perhaps foretelling that which is to come, and was common in the classical Greek and Roman worlds. The idea—which was carried on into medieval times—usually referred to strange births in the natural world, where perfectly normal-seeming mothers gave birth to offspring that appeared inhuman. It was thought this was because the mother may have somehow "manufactured" a ghastly looking child through some action (or inaction) during her pregnancy. Thus, if she had ventured too near a horse and had become agitated or terrified by it, her child would acquire equine characteristics. It is interesting to note that this belief was still prevalent in the colloquial lore of 19th-century England. (The grotesque characteristics of the celebrated Elephant Man, John Merrick, were attributed to the fact that his pregnant mother had been startled by a circus elephant whilst she was carrying him.) Thus, in its original sense the monstrum might be the effect of external forces on the unborn child. The births of such children were invariably a sign of approaching evil and might foretell dark times for a family, a city, or even a country.

The second origin of the word may be the Latin term *monere* meaning "to warn." Particularly in medieval times when the Church often held sway, the births of such children might denote evil or impure actions on behalf of an individual or a community, and served as a warning to those all around to follow the precepts of a moral life. The appearance of such "monsters" was supposedly God "having a word" with the individuals or

societies in which they appeared and reminding them of their moral re-
sponsibilities. Once again such appearances were considered unnatural and
grotesque. But they were the work of God alone.

Gradually the idea of the monster became more flexible. Starting out
as a description of something that was strange and bizarre, it gradually
widened in its concept. During the 19th century it applied to "monster
spectacles" (or "freak shows" as they were sometimes more crudely named),
where physically unusual humans and rather strange animals were often
exhibited to the curious (and paying) public. Here were bearded women;
boneless boys from some exotic, far-away location; two-headed snakes;
and alligator dogs. A number of these were physically deformed or hand-
icapped; some were fakes but, as "monsters," they all had one thing in
common: they were part of the natural world. This was indeed stressed
by the showmen who located their birthplaces as being remote corners of
the world. Man-made creations, such as the Hydra of Hamburg, were of a
rather different order.

From earliest times, religions said that only God (or some form of Creator or Creators) could control the vital spark that was eventually fanned
into life. The creation of a living being was a great mystery, which was
denied to man and remained the sole prerogative of the Divine. And yet,
according to nearly all religions, the living world and all that existed within
it had been *made* by some external force or intelligence. For instance, in
the book of Genesis the Bible described how God had made the first man
out of clay ("the dust of the earth") using Divine powers. Jewish mythology stated that God had made several prototypes, using similar material,
before he got it correctly. Stories of Adam Kadmon and other such beings
permeated Semitic mythology and Jewish lore. Adopting a slightly more
racist and xenophobic note, ancient Chinese folklore stated how the first
men had been baked in an oven by the Supreme Being—again like clay or
bread—with the first set being burned (the African race), the second set
being underdone (the white race), and the last being a perfect golden color.

Whether they were made of dust, emerged from an egg, or were created out of weeds and flotsam, the thing that united all of these early creations was that they were created by a Supreme Intelligence, which existed far outside themselves. This was the basis of many religions and beliefs, and it answered the question, "Where did I/we come from?"

The Creation of Life

The creation of life by humans themselves, outside natural procreation (which was usually approved by the Divine Intelligence) lay beyond the bounds of religion and the general order of things, and was usually considered unthinkable in most circles. And yet, there were some who wondered if this might not be possible. How had the Supreme Creator actually *made* life, they wondered. Was it through certain skills, energies, or by certain words or incantations known only to the Creator? And, if this were so, might not men learn these techniques themselves and perhaps be able to create the vital spark of life like the gods? This was a question that perplexed the early mind and has continued down until the present day. However, there was a kind of caveat to this thinking. If men *were* to create life, then what sort of life would it be? What would it look like? Certainly in the early civilized world there was a kind of generalized consensus that it would probably be less than perfect. Only the gods or the Creator alone could create perfect life, and anything created by men must only be a pale imitation of that perfection. To be otherwise would be to usurp the power and status of the Supreme Being. That which was man-made, it was thought, would either be grotesque or inhuman—in other words, a monster.

And another question arose. Exactly *how* would such creatures—imperfect though they were—be created? Most creation myths had spoken of beings forged "from the dust of the earth," from clay, or from other inert materials. It would be difficult, argued the theorists, to simply create a living being out of swirling and inert dust or, say, the mud along the banks of a river; so how might it be achieved? Through a Word of Power used by the Creator? Through spells or incantations or magical symbols? (Jewish tradition said that there were several mysterious and secret books that held such information.) Through, as some alchemists argued, some form of secret chemical interaction? Through the harnessing of natural elements and forces? Could a living creation be *built* in the same way that men built a ship or a house?

This last question brought yet another notion into play. Not only was it considered as beyond the bounds of formal thinking to create life, but it was also believed to be beyond human powers to bring people back from the dead or to reanimate their bodies. This was only within the remit of certain specialized individuals—for example in Christian and Jewish terms that remit belonged to Jesus, the saints, and the patriarchs. If, as in the story of *Frankenstein,* a living being was built out of the various parts of the dead, how were these parts to be reinvigorated? Although it has its roots in actual scientific enquiry, the Frankenstein tradition is usually perceived as being connected to madness and sorcery, with a hint of diabolism. It is, after all, included among the "horror genre" of both books and films. The charnel elements surrounding the acquisition of the body parts for such a construction have only added to this macabre tradition.

As doctors began to investigate how the body worked during the 18th and 19th centuries, and as the knowledge of human anatomy grew, the idea of "building humans" from discarded body parts began to develop and expand. As we shall see, the idea of "cadaver construction" and the reanimation of the dead became the focus of much mainstream and peripheral scientific thought, and then became a kind of "holy grail" of science.

The idea of constructing sentient beings came into much sharper focus during the 20th century with the notion of robots and machine-men. Although there had been tales of metal men from classical times, these had simply been in the form of legends and fables, but in more modern times the idea began to take on a sharper significance. Science-fiction

stories portrayed human-like machines serving Mankind in futures of varying types—it is always interesting to note that these machine-men were
always somehow less than actual men, and that they always functioned in
a subservient role—many of them in a humanoid shape (arms, legs, and
heads). Many such stories concerned these machines turning against their
human masters and inflicting some sort of harm upon them—becoming,
as it were, monsters within their own right.

As science progressed through the 20th century and into the 21st, the
concept of cloning and the development of artificial life from cells became
more and more pronounced. With both medical and scientific advances
the concept of actually creating life suddenly became more viable. But
somewhere in the back of the human psyche the old medieval warning
reasserted itself. The creation of life should be for a Supreme Being (or
Beings) alone, and the monster that could be created, like the Hydra of
Hamburg, might terrify and threaten humanity. Even today the idea of
cloning and life-creation from cells is approached with a fair amount of
caution and indeed opposition in certain quarters.

And yet the idea of humans creating at least some form of living entity
independent of nature or of some Divine Being hasn't gone away, and in
many ways it still remains a "holy grail" of enquiry. But neither has the idea
that such a creation would be far less than perfect—that it would indeed be
a monster. And the stories that have been passed down across the generations only serve to illustrate that fundamental point. All were beings with
the innate ability to turn on Mankind if they so chose. They were truly
things of which to be terrified. And with the actual dawning of scientific
cloning, the idea of a species of genetically constructed humans or animals
seems to have moved a step closer. The concept of creating monstrous life,
once the province of sorcerers and dark alchemists, now seems to be the
domain of the scientist. And still, like the monk-created Hydra, such an
idea has the power to shock and terrify.

But who or what were these manufactured beings? Were (or *are)* they as terrifying as we might think? And what were their origins? And are they warnings of things that might be to come? Perhaps it is time to explore the dark regions of the mind where they dwell and take a fresh look at these man-made monstrosities, both real and imagined. It's maybe now time to let the children of clay emerge from the shadows.

THE HORROR OF FRANKENSTEIN

GRANT ME A FIGURE, TALL AND SPARE,
THE SPEED OF THE ELK, THE CLAWS OF A BEAR,
THE POISON OF SNAKES, THE WIT OF A FOX,
THE STEALTH OF A WOLF, THE STRENGTH OF AN OX
THE JAWS OF A TIGER, THE TEETH OF A SHARK,
THE EYES OF A CAT THAT SEES IN THE DARK.

—AN ALLEGED MAGICAL CREATION INVOCATION

PROBABLY NO CREATURE typifies the idea of the man-made monster more aptly than the figure of Frankenstein, which appears in the novel of the same name, first published in 1818 and written by Mary Wollstonecraft Shelley, the wife of the poet Percy Bysshe Shelley. Although the name *Frankenstein* has often been attached to the shambling man-like shape

made from reconstructed and reanimated body parts, the being itself is actually nameless, but nevertheless takes the name of its creator Victor Frankenstein.

Shelley's novel portrays Victor Frankenstein as an arrogant, egocentric individual with a prodigious intellect who is obsessed with his own brilliance, imagining himself to have almost God-like abilities. He is widely read—mainly old alchemical volumes such as those by Cornelius Agrippa, Paracelsus, and Albertus Magnus, which he feels still have relevance is his modern world—and has become obsessed with the "secret of life," which is hinted at in several of these tomes. At the University of Ingolstadt in Bavaria, where he goes to study, Victor proves to be an exceptional scholar but, as he attempts to marry the ideas of the ancient alchemists with those of more modern science, he is laughed at and mocked. In a fit of anger, he returns to his family's castle in order to conduct clandestine experiments to create a being for himself. He employs servants to bring him parts of bodies—mainly from executed criminals—which he puts together to create a gigantic man-like figure. This he brings to life through the medium of electricity, diverted from a passing storm. However, that which he creates has the strength of many men but the mind of a child.

The being that Victor unleashes on the world is clearly a monster. Approximately 8 feet tall, it is ugly, with translucent, yellow skin—the rotting flesh of the dead—that "barely disguised the workings of the vessels and muscles underneath," with glowing eyes, black hair and lips, and white teeth. Although Shelley sought to describe him as a man, perhaps the most abiding image of the creature is the one taken from James Whale's 1931 film *Frankenstein* with Boris Karloff in the title role and with makeup by Jack Pierce. The actual creation of the "Frankenstein look" remains controversial, because Whale stated that Pierce had only been following suggestions made by him. Pierce, of course, stated that the image was his idea. Whoever created it, Karloff made the look his own, and it has formed the basis for many subsequent adaptations of the monster. We are all familiar with the bulky, grotesque, shambling figure with its slightly elongated and bulbous head and face; its hideous stitched and surgically scarred features; its bolted-together neck; and its hooded eyes and neck spikes where electrodes might have been attached. It wears a dark suit, which is clearly far too short, thus exaggerating long arms that end in surgically scarred hands. The look is completed with heavy workman-like boots, which only serve to give it a clumsy, stiff-legged walk. Although there have been several attempts to "modernize" the monster by making it appear slightly more human, this is the image that most of us retain.

Victor cannot control his creation, which escapes and wanders abroad in the surrounding countryside. Here it demonstrates the patchwork of characteristics that created its personality. It can, for example, show great love, and it attaches itself to the family of a blind peasant—who cannot see its ugliness—and learns a rudimentary form of speech by secretly listening as the old, sightless man teaches his Arabic daughter-in-law to speak French. On the other hand, it kills a small boy who is terrified of its appearance. Innately horrified by its own act, it swears vengeance on humanity and upon Victor who created it.

The two—creation and creator—face each other on the top of a desolate mountain; rather than attack Victor, the creature demands that the scientist listen to his plight. It demands that Victor now create a mate for him so that he can live out his days like a normal man, albeit in isolation. Victor is horrified at the thought that this might create a species of such creatures that could one day threaten humanity itself, so he refuses. The creature flees, renewing his vow to destroy Victor and declaring ominously, "I will be with you on your wedding night."

On Victor Frankenstein's wedding night, the monster once again appears and kills his best friend, Henry Clerval, and also his bride, Elizabeth Lavenza. The double tragedy causes Victor's father, Alphonse, to die of grief. The monster that Victor created has effectively ruined his world. Now it is Victor who is consumed with rage and hatred, and he vows to hunt the creature down, wherever it might be, and destroy it. He pursues it to the Arctic Circle where Victor loses control of a dog sled and plunges into freezing Arctic waters. He manages to save himself from drowning and is found, near to death, by members of an expedition. Suffering from acute pneumonia, Victor relates the entire incredible tale to Captain Robert Walton, the expedition leader, who is not sure whether he can believe him or not. Before Walton can question him further Victor succumbs to the fever and dies. Later, the creature manages to board the expedition vessel, intent on fulfilling its revenge, only to find itself thwarted. Its creator is already dead. In frustration, it curses humanity once more and announces its intention to go to the uttermost ends of the earth, burn itself, and die. It leaps into the Arctic Ocean and is never seen again.

Since then there have been many additions to the Frankenstein tale as writers and film directors have sought to extend it. Reference has already been made to James Whale's *Frankenstein* in 1931, and he directed another Frankenstein movie in 1935, *The Bride of Frankenstein* (which built upon the creature's wish, in the original tale, for a mate). There is also Earl C. Kenton's *Ghost of Frankenstein* (1942), *House of Frankenstein* (1944), Richard Lee's *Son of Frankenstein* (1939), Roy McNeill's *Frankenstein Meets the Wolf Man* (1943), and *Abbot and Costello Meet Frankenstein* directed by Charles Barton in 1948, all from Universal Studios. All these together with subsequent movies and countless books served to firm both the notion and image of the Frankenstein monster in the public psyche.

Mary Shelley

But how did the idea come about?

Mary Shelley was born Mary Godwin in 1797, the daughter of two celebrated intellectuals of the day—William Godwin and Mary Wollstonecraft. She grew up in an unconventional household where poets and thinkers came and went. One of these was the poet Percy Bysshe Shelley with whom she formed a relationship, eventually marrying him in 1816 when his first wife died. Her life remained unconventional—her husband had a mistress Jane Clairmont (who later called herself Claire), who actually lived with them—and was compounded by her husband's friendship with the talented Lord Byron. In 1816, this entourage set out for a holiday in Switzerland, accompanied by Byron's physician, Dr. John William Polidori. They took a chalet on the shores of Lake Geneva, not far from the Villa Diodati. There, on a particularly stormy night, Byron challenged them all to write a ghost story in keeping with the elements outside.

At this literary session Polidori is supposed to have written the first vampire story in English—*The Vampire* (later erroneously attributed to Byron)—but it is for Mary Shelley's contribution that the gathering is chiefly remembered. Fascinated by her husband and Byron's discussion about galvanic electricity—a form of electricity that was supposed to generate within and power the body—Mary wrote down part of a first draft of *Frankenstein*, which she intended to be no more than a short story. However, the themes contained in the tale intrigued both Mary and her husband, and throughout 1817, she developed the tale in the countryside at Marlow in England and created the novel. Throughout the years, there were many other publications of the book, each one adding to the myth and the horror of Frankenstein's man-created monster. Shelley herself added a subtitle to the overall title—"A Modern Prometheus," which may give some idea of her own insight into the character of the creature.

Prometheus

In classical Greek mythology, Prometheus (the name means "forethought") was one of the Titans, the son of Iaptus and Themis, and according to some versions of the creation tale was charged, together with his brother Epimethus (meaning "afterthought") with the creation of men and animals. Prometheus created men out of clay and Epimethus created the animals. However, Prometheus wasn't terribly pleased with his creation—the humans were weak and miserable things that went about on all fours. As all the attributes from the gods had been used up by his brother in giving the animals protection from the world, Prometheus resolved to give Mankind something special. Being something of a rogue and a trickster, he was able to steal a spark of Divine fire from the table of Zeus and took it to Earth to give to his creations. This gave men both heat and light and enabled them to walk upright, similar to the gods themselves, and began civilization as we know it. The gods, however, were not pleased—Zeus captured Prometheus and chained him to a rock where his liver and intestines were eaten by a vulture, and then they were constantly renewed. Thus, Prometheus lived in perpetual pain. This was the image that Mary Shelley sought to convey in her tale: a broken creator overwhelmed by the thing (or situation) that he'd created.

Origins of Frankenstein

Of course as with any major tale, the novel reflected all the concerns and alarms of the day, and although I do not propose to go into the allegories and subtexts that it contains I do intend to probe a little deeper into the idea of the monster.

For example, did the tale have any basis in reality? Although Victor Frankenstein is regarded as one of the earliest examples of what is now known as "the mad scientist," was he actually based on someone who had attempted a similar experiment? Might somebody have tried to create such a creature as the Frankenstein monster or perhaps bring the dead back to life using scientific means? And if so, who?

The times in which Mary Shelley wrote were rather tumultuous from an ideological perspective. It was a time when the last vestiges of superstition were slowly disappearing, and a new scientific light was beginning to dawn on western Europe. The two traditions—the old notion of alchemy (which in many respects bordered on magic in the popular mind) and the scientific rigor—merged together in the common perspective, and such an amalgam forms the basis of Mary Shelley's novel. Alongside the interest in scientific methodology lay the works of the early thinkers on magic, such as Paracelsus and Albertus Magnus—writers whom Victor Frankenstein avidly read. Indeed, in the book, he successfully blends the alchemical tradition with that of electricity and "modern" science in the creation of his creature. In a sense he is a man of his time. If he did have a base in fact just who might he have been?

The name *Frankenstein* gives us little clue other than to establish the scientist's noble status—an important factor in Mary Shelley's day. The name simply means "rock or hill of the Franks" and refers to a location in West Germany that may have been the site of a hill fort constructed by the ancient Frankish peoples who were an indigenous Germanic people. In many films, Frankenstein appears as a "baron," but the Frankensteins never held such rank—they were, in fact, landgraves (substantial landowners), a title that was just as powerful. They traced their ancestry from ancient German nobles. In 1250 Lord Konrad II Reiz von Breuberg built a castle near Darmstadt, Germany, which he called "Burg Frankenstein" (Castle Frankenstein), and from then on added the title "von und zu Frankenstein" to his name. Documents drawn up in 1252 show that he and his family now used the name "the Knights Frankenstein" and that they maintained a Free Imperial Lordship (which meant that they had only to answer to the Holy Roman Emperor himself), as well as substation land holdings that stretched as far as Hesse. In 1292, their territory became part of the lands of the Counts of Katzenelnbogen to whom they opened the courts and tried to form an uneasy alliance. However, the knights were riven with internal dissentions between various members of the Frankenstein family and bloody feuds were common. In 1363, Castle Frankenstein was divided into two parts, each held by a different part of the family between whom relations seemed to be strained, but in the late 15th century only one branch of the Knights Frankenstein possessed it, and it extended and enlarged the fortress. In 1662, the Lord Frankenstein, Johannes I, sold his lordship to the Landgraves of Hesse-Darmstadt after various lawsuits between members of his family, and the Knights Frankenstein died out. In the 1680s the castle became a hospital and a refuge for locals fleeing from the armies of the French king Louis XIV as they rampaged through the countryside before later falling into ruin. Victor Frankenstein (had he existed) would therefore have been descended from a noble and military line, and might have been extremely wealthy, but that would probably be his family's only connection to the legend.

There may be, however, one connection to the Frankenstein tale of which Mary Shelley may have been aware. In 1673, the castle was the birthplace of Johann Conrad Dippel, a controversial theologian and al-chemist (some would say, black magician) who came and went there from time to time during succeeding years. Dippel may well have been related in some way to the Frankensteins, but if he was, the nature of his familial link is not known. However, he used their name when it suited him. It has always been suggested that he was the template for Victor Frankenstein in Mary Shelley's story, but the facts about his life are so vague, and just how much Shelley would have known about him is open to question, so the issue is questionable. We will look more closely at Dippel a little later, but perhaps a more profitable avenue might be to look at another scientist about whom Mary Shelley would almost certainly have heard.

Giovanni Aldini

Giovanni Aldini was born into a wealthy and noble family in Bologna, Italy, in 1762. His family was indeed an illustrious one, for he was the brother of a senior Italian statesman, Count Antonio Aldini, Secretary of State for the Kingdom of Italy and advisor to Napoleon on Italian matters. More importantly, he was also the nephew of the medical scientist Luigi Galvini, whose work he championed. Galvini had noticed that the limbs of frogs seemed to move spontaneously when subjected to a spark of electricity. This formed the theory (published in 1791 and edited by his nephew Giovanni

Aldini) of "galvanic electricity" or "animal electricity." Put simply, this postulated the idea that the muscles of all living animals were powered by a certain form of natural electricity that circulated through their bodies. Both the source and the generation of this form of electricity lay within chemical reactions, which were constantly occurring within the body. It was thought that such reactions did not stop, even with death, and so it might be possible to restimulate them in the moments after a body had expired and restart the muscles (including the heart). It might be possible, it was argued, to bring life back to the dead.

The idea fascinated Aldini and he was determined to prove it. The movements of individual parts of dead animals when excited by electricity—what today we might describe as "muscular spasms" brought on by the electrical current—seemed to bear out his uncle's theory. However, there was one difference between Galvini and Aldini: the former was a studious scholar; the latter was something of a showman. And, although a professor of physics at Bologna University (appointed in 1798), Aldini still engaged in "shows" and "diversions" in order to raise money for his proposed experiments. Many of these concerned electricity and were designed to entice his wealthy audience to invest in some of his wilder scientific activities. It is difficult for us to conceive that this was a world in which electricity was an extremely novel and terrifying concept, and the sight of a severed dog, sheep, or monkey head moving and twitching involuntarily or opening and closing its eyes was enough to cause wonder and awe in most people. And Aldini seems to have been the consummate showman, building a fevered expectation in his audience and then producing "terrifying" results to gasps of wonder and admiration. He would even charge his own body with electrical current and throw bolts of electricity from his fingertips in a spectacular arc across a darkened room to the astonishment of onlookers.

Aldini's central theory, however, and the idea that motivated many of his experiments, was that galvanic electricity might be used to bring people back from the dead. Galvanic electricity might stimulate the heart—which

was after all no more than a large muscle—and this provided the flicker of new life. This, he argued, would benefit the military—soldiers shot dead on the battlefield might be revived by his process and would thus be able to fight again. However, in order to prove the theory, he needed fresh corpses on which to conduct his experiments, and possibly the best method of obtaining these was to use the bodies of recently executed criminals supplied by the authorities. But here lay a problem. In Italy, criminals were executed by beheading, and a decapitated body was of little use to Aldini, as he needed his corpses to be intact and whole. It was all very well to have the twitching head of a murderer hung between strands of electrical power in one of his "spectacles," but such a show had little actual scientific merit. Most European countries followed Italy and used decapitation as a means of execution, but there was one country that did not: England. English law favoured hanging as a means of executing its criminals, and this suited Aldini's purposes admirably.

In January 1802 Aldini performed an experiment on an executed criminal in Bologna. The man had been beheaded and the experiment was only a tentative one, but even so the scientist appeared to get the lungs and heart to work, if only momentarily. This fired his enthusiasm, convincing him that he was right and that he should pursue further investigations with a fresh and whole corpse. He applied unsuccessfully to the Italian authorities for a whole body and made up his mind to leave Italy and conduct his experiments elsewhere.

So in December 1802, Giovanni Aldini arrived in London with the intention of bringing some of the English dead back to life. At the time, the English capital was at the center of medicine and science, but it was also a violent and dangerous place. However, it was also very wealthy and a possible source of great patronage for the Italian scientist. Aldini set about winning such patronage from the cream of London society by a series of "diversions" and shows, just as he had back in Bologna. One of the bodies that he had to interest was the Royal College of Surgeons, which contained some of the foremost and most influential medical men of the day.

Ever the showman, he began to make his performances more and more spectacular, dramatic, and laden with mystery. One of the most famous of his "diversions" was known as "Kissing the Electrical Venus," in which a young lady stood on an insulated block and was mildly charged with electrical current. Young men then came forward to kiss her and received a gentle shock as they did so. In some cases, even a tiny tongue of current came from her lips, which was very effective in a darkened room. Aldini was soon drawing the crowds—and, more importantly, interest in himself and his experiments amongst the wealthy. But such shows were only a prelude to his real business in London: conducting experiments that would reanimate the dead.

Besides the wealthy and influential of London society there was one other person whom Aldini needed to make his experiments work. That was somebody who could supply him with a fresh corpse (or corpses) for him to experiment upon. In this regard he was extremely fortunate to make the acquaintance of the mysterious Mr. Pass.

Mr. Pass

Little is known about Mr. Pass (even his Christian name is unclear) and he remains a shadowy and rather sinister figure. What *is* known is that he was the Beadle of the Royal College of Surgeons and he was certainly a very influential man in certain quarters. Normally a Beadle held the rank of Parish Constable charged with charitable works on behalf of the Church and local authorities (the word is derived from the Latin *bidellus* meaning "herald"—one who summoned the local householders together in ancient times). However, in Hebrew, the word *shammash* or *gabbai* could be used, meaning "man of all work" or "caretaker," and perhaps this description more aptly fitted Mr. Pass. He was a sort of generalized "fixer" who looked after the needs of the surgeons of the Royal College (there is even a suggestion that he might have been a failed surgeon himself, although this is not actually certain). One of the tasks he performed was to obtain dead bodies from the gallows, used for dissection in the training of young doctors. However, such bodies were frequently in short supply, and under the law the number for which Mr. Pass might apply was strictly limited—in normal circumstances, he could claim no more than three from any one court session. It is highly probable that he dealt with men known as Resurrectionists or "Sack-em-ups"—body-snatchers who looted graves and sold their contents to the medical profession for a substantial profit. Mr. Pass may have carried out a lucrative trade in dead bodies.

The bodies the Resurrectionists acquired were of little use to Aldini. It was usually about two or three days before it was safe for the body-snatchers to exhume the corpse, and by that time a process of decay had already set in. Aldini needed bodies that were fresh—a few hours after death, rather than several days old. Ideally what he desired was a corpse that had just been cut down from the gallows. He insisted that this corpse be in healthy condition, and he instructed Mr. Pass to find him one. The Beadle did not wholly disappoint.

It appears that Mr. Pass had connections in Newgate Jail. The prison housed a variety of inmates, from those who had found themselves in serious debt, to murderers and highwaymen. Deaths and executions occurred there on a fairly regular basis. Most of them, however, failed to meet Aldini's rigid specifications. In many cases they were emaciated (prisoners were often required to pay for their own upkeep while incarcerated and many could not afford to eat, or were riddled with the various diseases that swept through the unsanitary gaol). If his experiment was to be the success that he anticipated, Aldini required a healthy and robust specimen. Mr. Pass was able to find him one—but with one significant drawback.

George Foster

George Foster (or Forster) was a journeyman coachbuilder, a skilled but lowly profession. Like many of the teeming mass that inhabited the city of London he and his wife Jane were desperately poor. So poor, in fact, that they could not afford to live together but contented themselves with seeing each other every Sunday. They had two children in the city work-house, another dead, and the youngest—a baby girl, named Louisa—still living with her mother. They were trying desperately to keep the infant out of the workhouse, but it was proving increasingly difficult. Jane was subject to fits of depression during which she drank, and the tiny family struggled. However, each Sunday, George would invariably make his way down to the Thames, close to where Jane and Louisa lived, in order to see them and give them what money he could.

On December 6, 1802, John Atkins—a Thames boatman—made a horrible and tragic discovery beneath the prow of his boat. The body of an infant girl was floating in the water and had lodged close to the riverbank. Further up, Atkins found the drowned body of the dead child's mother. A washerwoman who lived close by identified them as Jane and Louisa Foster. Police were called, and on investigation it seemed that the pair might have been murdered.

Suspicion immediately fell on Jane's husband. The two had been seen together the previous Sunday along the towpath close to the river, and an-other washerwoman claimed that she had seen them arguing. When first questioned Foster declared his innocence, and although he admitted seeing Jane on the previous Sunday, he stated that both she and the baby had been alive when he'd left them. However, a number of other witnesses started to come forward stating that they'd either seen or heard the couple arguing and Foster threatening his wife; the case against him was starting to look bad. On December 21, George Foster was arrested for the murder of his wife and child.

Foster's defense was rambling and contradictory. Quite possibly a man of limited intelligence, he became easily confused when subjected to inten-sive questioning. Yes, he and Jane had quarrelled over money, but they had been on good terms when he'd left. He kept pleading his innocence but the authorities still suspected him of murder. He was thrown into Newgate Jail to await trial. Although the evidence against him was circumstantial, it was highly likely that he'd be sentenced and executed.

George Foster fitted Aldini's specifications perfectly. He was a young man in his prime, and years of building the bodywork of coaches had made him exceptionally fit and muscular. His outdoor work had made him healthy and his body looked to be in perfect shape. There was only one problem: he hadn't been sentenced to death yet. Aldini had to wait. In the meantime, he redoubled his efforts in attracting wealthy London sponsors. He ran ever more dramatic "spectaculars" in the city's salons and frequented the clubs where the cream of society hung out. One of those clubs that he courted was the Royal Humane Society—a group that represented the pinnacle of medical, scientific, and social influence. If he could win the backing of the society, then there would be no limit to what he might achieve in London.

He also approached the Maritime Office of the Royal Navy with a startling proposition. At the time England was engaged in a war with France— a war in which the main theater of conflict was the ocean. A number of sea battles had been fought with a significant loss of life due to drowning. Aldini's proposition was that if drowned bodies could be recovered, he could stimulate them with galvanic electricity and bring them back to life. They could then return to the war. It sounded like the mythical Cauldron of Goibu in Celtic legend. The Navy was intrigued and showed at least a passing interest. The Italian was certainly the talk of London and was provoking intense speculation about the possible success of his experiments.

But apart from distracting the upper echelons of London society, Aldini needed to keep George Foster in good shape if he was to complete his most fantastic experiment, and this task he entrusted to Mr. Pass. Each day, the Beadle would visit Newgate Jail, bringing food and drink for the prisoner as he awaited his trial. Things were not looking good for the journeyman coachbuilder—although there was no hard evidence to connect him with the deaths of his wife and child, the police were still building up a case against him based largely on hearsay and speculation, which they planned to take to court. If found guilty he would certainly hang. And there was something else—something that terrified George Foster beyond words.

The Murder Act passed by the English Parliament in 1754 held one other horror for the condemned—the threat of dissection. The bodies of criminals who had been convicted of murder were liable, at the discretion of the court (and it was seldom refused), to have their bodies cut up for surgical investigation—usually for the purposes of demonstration by the medical colleges of the city. George Foster was a religious man. He believed that if his body were to be dissected, he would be refused entry to Heaven at the Final Judgment when the dead were raised, intact and whole, to stand before God. If his body were to be cut into a hundred pieces—as he assumed would be the case—then he could never hope to attain Paradise and see Jane or Louisa again. It was here that Mr. Pass stepped in. If Foster were to sign his body over to Aldini as a next of kin, the Italian would ensure that it would not fall foul of the anatomist's knife. Even so, there was no guarantee that he would be spared anatomization even if he signed. This was part of the law, but it gave Aldini a useful lever to use if the execution took place.

But the case against George Foster was weak and relied on dubious evidence, some of which was blatantly manufactured by the police. For example, one of the chief witnesses against Foster was Sarah Daniels, a 9-year-old girl who had been friendly with Jane Foster and who had been traumatized by her death. She claimed to have heard the argument between Jane and her husband and the threats that were issued. When she was taken to identify Foster, the police told her that she was "going to see the murderer," and so when Foster appeared in the dock at his trial, she identified him as such. Foster did little more than declare his innocence. He had stayed with Jane on the Saturday night and they had gone for a walk the next day when they had argued over money. But he left her at 3 p.m. and had gone to see his two other children in the Whetstone Workhouse before going home. (He would later contradict this, saying that he had set out for Whetstone, but had turned for home due to the failing light before he actually got to the workhouse.) He had not murdered her, he insisted, but he didn't provide an alibi for himself. There is some suggestion that Aldini or Mr. Pass may have had some influence on the way that the questioning was carried out in order to paint Foster in the worst possible light and so secure a conviction. This was essential if his experiment was to be carried out—time was running against Aldini, and if Foster wasn't convicted, the chances of procuring another suitable body were slim. In Newgate, Foster sank into a deep melancholy and Mr. Pass was despatched to reassure him that things were not as bad as they seemed, to keep his spirits up, and most of all to encourage him to eat and to stay healthy.

On January 12, 1803, George Foster appeared in court. If the case against him was weak, his own defense was even weaker, relying simply on character witnesses. His lack of alibi was repeatedly drawn to the jury's attention, and although he said he had been in Whetstone around the time of Jane and Louisa's death, he brought nobody forward to corroborate this. Public opinion had turned against him—it was not only the murder of his wife of which he was accused, but also the murder of an infant, which in everybody's eyes was a hideous crime. Although there is no direct evidence that Aldini affected the outcome of the case, he had sufficient influence among the upper reaches of London society to gain access to the judicial system. Under the direction of the judge, the jury arrived at their verdict. George Foster was guilty of murder on all counts. The judge did not delay in pronouncing the sentence. Foster was to be hanged by the neck until dead. Giovanni Aldini had his experimental specimen.

Although Foster's body had been signed over to him, the Italian was still not sure that it would escape the anatomist's knife. He despatched Mr. Pass to bribe the Newgate authorities to deliver the corpse into his hands at the Royal College of Surgeons shortly after the hanging. In the meantime, Foster sank deeper into despair and was now subject to fits of grief and rage during which times he was almost uncontrollable. It was during one of these fits that he attempted to take his own life, using some sharp instrument that he had somehow procured. This was not uncommon among many condemned prisoners in Newgate—after all, they had nothing to lose and it was an attempt to take control of their own fate. Foster's attempt seems to have been fairly serious and it was enough to bring Mr. Pass hurrying to the prison to revive him. The execution date had been set for three days after the trial, and it was essential that Foster be kept alive and in good physical condition for the experiment that would take place directly after.

The prisoner now refused to eat and was growing steadily weaker. Mr. Pass had to attempt to force-feed him as he lay in his cell in order to keep some sort of strength up—a malnourished corpse was no use to Aldini. In fact, on the morning of his execution (January 16, 1803), he was so weak that he had to be carried from his cell by two warders and helped up the steps of the scaffold, which he "was unable to mount." Before the hanging, Foster is said to have made a full confession to the murder of his wife and child. Again this was not uncommon among the condemned, and in Foster's case there is some question as to whether such a confession was actually made or not. The act of execution was carried out quite speedily, with Mr. Pass standing by; however, the body was ordered to hang for at least an hour to ensure that Foster was dead; Mr. Pass waited anxiously nearby.

Whilst Foster was being hanged, Aldini was preparing a gloomy basement room in the Royal College of Surgeons for the supreme experiment of his career. He had set up a bank of galvanic batteries and connection equipment all through the low chamber and had even tested the electrodes he planned to use on himself. He had invited some of the most prominent men in London—including representatives of the medical profession and from the Navy—to see his "revitalization experiment." Everything had to be right and the experiment had to be successful.

On January 17, 1803, Aldini's audience assembled. Foster's body was brought in by Mr. Pass and was laid out on a slab in the middle of the galvanic batteries, which were now fully charged. Aldini placed the electrodes on the temples of the corpse and adjusted a mild electrical flow. The fingers of the dead man moved in response and the eyes flickered open, revealing fixed pupils beyond. This, of course, had been a prelude, and, still playing the showman, Aldini now moved to the main part of his experiment. One electrode was attached to Foster's temple, another was placed in his rectum, and the power was increased. The corpse jumped and arched its back; the face grimaced horribly as the muscles contracted. More power was administered. It is difficult to convey the tension that must have filled the room, which was lit only by candlelight and oil lamps. Aldini's audience must have wondered if the thing in front of them might do more than arch its back or flex its fingers; might it rise from the slab and move among them? Aldini poured more power into it and the corpse moved and thrashed. Then suddenly, as if in response to the flood of electric current, the chest rose and fell as if the dead man was taking a single breath. This was what Aldini was waiting for, and he motioned his audience closer, although few dared to do so. However, there was no second breath and the body lay motionless under their gaze. In a frenzy now, Aldini poured more galvanic electricity into the body, making it thrash and move, but already the lungs were starting to deflate and there was no further response. The audience could see that the experiment was a failure and were already starting to drift away. Aldini begged them to wait, but they were already gone; the Italian and Mr. Pass were alone in the basement chamber with Foster's dead body. In an unutterable rage, Aldini wrecked the equipment that he'd so painstakingly set up, pulling the galvanic batteries to the floor and snapping all the connections. Then, it is said, telling Mr. Pass to clean up, he left.

The next morning Mr. Pass was found dead in the basement room. To this day, his death remains unexplained, although the official records state that he "died of fright," most probably from a seizure. Significantly, George Foster's body, which was still on the slab, had been moved (or, some speculated, had moved itself?). What had happened? Who had killed the enigmatic Mr. Pass? There were suggestions that Aldini had fatally struck the Beadle in a blind fit of rage at the failure of his experiment—if this was the truth, then the Italian had enough contacts in the upper reaches of London society to get the story squashed. The main consensus is that the process Mr. Pass had witnessed—the galvanization of Foster's body—had so frightened Mr. Pass that it had brought on a fatal seizure. But there were also those who believed that perhaps the body of George Foster had risen briefly from its slab and had terrified the Beadle, bringing on the seizure. Could it be, they asked, that Aldini's experiment had actually worked? Had the corpse then fallen back? This, of course, is simply gruesome speculation.

Giovanni Aldini left London defeated and went to France, where he tried to ingratiate himself with members of the French National Institute without much success. Returning to Italy, he published a lavish account at the end of 1803, which was also published in London, and was entitled "An Account of the Late Improvements in Galvanism with a series of curious and interesting experiments before the Commission of the French National Institute and repeated lately in the anatomical theatres of London by John Aldini." John Aldini was of course himself, Giovanni. In florid language he detailed his work and blamed the circumstances in which he had attempted to resurrect Foster's body for the failure of his experiment: The body was not completely intact by virtue of attempted suicide, it was malnourished, and the situation had not been conductive, even for the greatest scientist of his day. Aldini was not a man to sell himself short. The book generated a great deal of interest in academic circles, and in honor of his work Aldini was awarded the Order of the Iron Crown and was made a councillor of Milan by the emperor of Austria. He remained in Milan until his death in 1834, leaving quite a substantial fortune behind. Although he sometimes performed some of his "distractions" using galvanic electricity, he never again attempted the same experiment he'd done in that gloomy basement of the Royal College of Surgeons.

There was one final, tragic twist in George Foster's story. Several days after he'd been hanged two women approached a London clergyman with new evidence in the case. They knew Jane Foster very well and stated that during her fits of depression, she had frequently said that she would "make away with herself." She had also said that she would take the infant girl with her as "she could not bear to be parted from her." They attested that on the morning before she met her husband, Jane had been in a particularly depressed state concerning money. It seems possible, therefore, that while in a disturbed state of mind, Jane Foster took her own life as well as that of her baby daughter, and that George was indeed innocent of their murders. The information, of course, came too late to save him, but it is eminently possible that had it been known earlier it would have spared Jane's husband the hangman's noose and denied Aldini his specimen.

Although the actual experiment had been a failure, Aldini was successful in one respect. He had London both talking about and interested in galvanic electricity and its possibilities. And it brought the idea of restimulation of life together with the resurrection of the dead very much to the fore. Aldini's own book, which circulated in both London and Europe in 1804 and 1805, generated something of a "buzz" with its radical ideas. And Mary Shelley would, of course, have been acutely aware of such discussion and of the ideas that it entailed. A stream of thinkers and writers came to her father's house to debate and query many of the current ideological and scientific positions, and there is little doubt that the question of galvanic electricity would have been among them. One of the visitors to the house would have been Dr. Henry Cline, who for a number of years was William Godwin's physician. He took a keen interest in both the scientific and medical advances of the day. Indeed, Cline was Mary's own personal doctor during her early years and had become a close friend. In 1814—two years before she first began to pen *Frankenstein*—the doctor had been involved in a rather notable medical case. Using a modicum of galvanic electricity, he had managed to revive a sailor who had been lying in a coma for several months. Whether or not the man had come out of the coma voluntarily or whether this had been due to Cline stimulating him is unclear, but the incident provoked great medical interest at the time. It was, in fact, as if the man had risen from the dead. Cline himself had become something of a celebrity, and the incident had again provoked the debate about resurrection from beyond the grave.

Percy Bysshe Shelley

Henry Cline was not the only medical man who may have inspired Mary Shelley and served as a model for Victor Frankenstein. Between 1809 and 1810, Percy Bysshe Shelley had formed a friendship with an elderly gentleman named James Lind. From him, according to Shelley, the poet had acquired "a taste for chemistry and chemical experiments." Although he was by that time an old man, Lind had a medical background (having been a ship's surgeon), had traveled extensively in places such as China, and was especially interested in new medical and scientific discoveries. He was especially knowledgeable on galvanism. In fact, between 1782 and 1809 he had frequently corresponded with both the London-based Italian scientist Tiberio Cavallo and also Dr. Joseph Banks, president of the Royal Society, regarding the stimulation of the nerves of dissected frogs using electrical current. Shelley described him as being the next best thing to an alchemist, both in appearance and temperament, and portrayed his study as being littered with mysterious and almost alchemical apparatus including galvanic batteries. Indeed, he based the character of Zonoras, the wise alchemist/ magician in his poem *Prince Athanese*, upon Lind. Although James Lind died in 1812, his memory lived on in Mr. Shelley's memory as a mentor and would undoubtedly have been conveyed to his wife.

With the background of her father's visitors and correspondents (which included Erasmus Darwin, father of Charles) and her husband's interest in galvanic experiments—in fact we know from her diaries that both Shelley and Byron had frequently discussed its properties during their time near the Villa Deodati—it is no wonder that Mary Shelley envisaged the lumbering figure of the monster made from "resurrected materials." But there is also one other figure that she may have known about, although his connection to the Frankenstein legend may have been slightly exaggerated. He is, however, an intriguing figure nonetheless.

Johann Konrad Dippel

Johann Konrad Dippel was born at Castle Frankenstein in 1673 and was connected to a branch of the factious Frankenstein family. In fact, he occasionally used the appellation *Frankenstiena* to his own name and at University may have been occasionally known as *Frankensteina-Strataemontanus.* He was a scholar and philosopher who took great interest in the fluctuating religious theories of the period, particularly in his own geographical area where the differing perspectives of Lutheran and Calvinist thought strove for supremacy. Dippel was educated at Giessen University in Germany, which, at the time, was in the forefront of the Lutheran school of thought, taking his Master's degree in theology in 1693. Although principally a theologian, it is rumoured that whilst at University, Dippel also studied alchemy, and it is known that he was intensely interested in science, especially in certain forms of chemistry. Rather than being a full-blown alchemist of the medieval type, Dippel may have dabbled in science as some of the wealthier men of the day were wont to do. It is also almost certain that, like Victor Frankenstein, he read some of the old books of dark philosophy and occultism such as by Paracelsus and Albertus Magnus. In many ways, he was comparable to an Irish counterpart, Gerald Fitzgerald the Great Earl of Desmond (the 15th Earl: 1533–1583), who probably dabbled in some form of elementary science, but who was also said to be a fearsome magician and warlock. This was propaganda put about by his enemies,

although the Earl (and presumably Dippel) did nothing to discourage it as it gave him certain kudos. Many reasonably wealthy men appear to have been fascinated by the "wisdom of the ancients" around this time and may have worked as amateur chemists, even sometimes teaching and lecturing in the subject. In fact, Dippel is said to have lectured briefly at the University of Strasbourg on both alchemy and chiromancy (fortune-telling) before the authorities revoked his licence to teach there, and he was obliged to move on, leaving something of a legend behind him. Much of his actual writings, however, are confined to religious themes, printing them under the name of Christians Democritus—part of his works under that name (originally published in Berleburg in 1743) still survive. Although he was the son of a Lutheran pastor, his books show a distinctly anti-Lutheran tone. He attacked the Church frequently, declaring it was much too guided by dogma and that true religion should have its foundations in brotherly love and self-sacrifice. Such views, especially in a largely Lutheran area of Germany, made him distinctly unpopular with those around him, and he was forced to move frequently from place to place.

Under the influence of the Saxon German theologian Gottfried Arnold, Dippel seems to have become a proponent of Pietistic Lutheranism, which was much more anti-dogmatic and millenarian in tone. Between 1700 and 1702, while living in the town of Offenbach, he engaged in a series of public and increasingly bitter disputes with another radical thinker and pastor, Conrad Broeske, whom he accused of being less than enthusiastic in embracing certain tenets of the Pietistic philosophy. Much of his diatribe against certain aspects of Lutheranism was printed on presses within Offenbach.

With his often wild and eccentric behavior, radical views, and love of alchemy, it's little wonder that Dippel attracted a great deal of attention and legend, some of it rather unwelcome. Like the Earl of Desmond, dark stories often grew up around him, particularly concerning the experiments he conducted. He was said, for example, to practice dark magic and necromancy. Dippel did little to stem such stories either by denying them or by modifying his behavior. Frequently short of money and in debt in his later years (he could never manage his own finances very well), he relied on his dubious reputation, making lavish promises about finding the Philosopher's Stone, the Holy Grail of ancient alchemists, which could allegedly turn base metal into gold. However, in religious Germany such promises were often viewed as an admission of dark sorcery, contrary to the laws of God.

But Dippel seems to have continued with his chemical experiments. He produced a creation called "Dippel's Oil"—made from ground-up animal bones, which was his equivalent for the "elixir of life." It was a noxious substance that had little to do with the extension of life, and its uses are now pretty much obsolete, although for a time it was used in sheep dips and as an insect repellent.

In 1704 while living in Berlin, Dippel, together with another chemist and dye manufacturer, Heinrich Diesbach, used the oil in the production of a red dye. To their surprise the dye turned a bluish color, becoming what was known as "Prussian Blue" or "Berlinner Blue." This seemed to be the pinnacle of Dippel's contribution to the alchemical art. Even so, the stories about his dark arts and weird experiments continued, as did his diatribes against formalized Lutheranism. It all served to make him a rather mysterious and controversial character.

At some point in his wanderings he may have returned to Castle Frankenstein. The area was heavily Lutheran, and while he was there, stories about him increased. Many may have been merged with old folktales from the area—the local historian and folklorist Walter Scheele argues that some of them may have been adaptations of stories collected by the Brothers Grimm—and bear little connection to Dippel at all. It was said, for example, that he had a secret laboratory there where he conducted strange and foul experiments with pieces of human remains and with cadavers that he had exhumed from local cemeteries. Such experiments were reputedly carried out under the supervision of the Devil himself. Even after Castle Franken-stein lay in ruins, strange lights were said to be seen there, and this was ascribed to Dippel working there. It was said that he had discovered the elixir of life and had somehow become immortal. This, of course, is only legend, and could certainly not have happened, as Dippel seems to have left Castle Frankenstein and returned to Berleburg where he is recorded as dying in 1734. Even after his death, many stories circulated about him, some trying to link him with Mary Shelley's novel and with the character of Victor Frankenstein. For example, it was said that he almost destroyed part of the central tower of the castle (where his laboratory was said to be located) using an early form of nitroglycerine. This is a glaring anachro-nism, because nitroglycerine was not invented at this time, and there is no record of the castle tower ever having been destroyed (which in itself would have been a significant event and worthy of note). It was said that he con-ducted experiments deep in his laboratory, which tried to move the soul of a dying man from one body to another; once again this may be no more than a fantastic tale similar to those ascribed to the ancient alchemists. There are also stories that say Dippel raided churchyards for bodies to use in his experiments and that he was hounded from the castle by locals as a necromancer and wizard. Again, there is really no evidence for this. Much of this seems to be a later addition—indeed, part of the legend concerning Dippel seems to have been inspired by the 20th-century film. In fact, there have even been suggestions that much of it was deliberately generated by filmmakers in order to give greater credibility to their movie and to provide talking points about it.

But there is no doubt that many creepy stories surrounded the figure of Johann Dippel, and it is possible that Mary Shelley may indeed have heard some of these when traveling through Switzerland. There is, however, no real evidence that she did actually visit Castle Frankenstein (which would have been in ruins at the time, although several attempts had been made to rebuild it). However, there is a suggestion that she actually did visit Darmstadt while traveling up the Rhine in 1814. But she would almost certainly have heard some dark stories of Dippel and about the internecine disputes surrounding the Frankenstein name, and this may have formed her vision both of the monster and of its creator.

Apart from Shelley's well-written and Gothically atmospheric work, and setting aside some of the intriguing characters that may have inspired her, why has the image of the lumbering monster exerted such a fascination on the human mind throughout the centuries? Perhaps it is the idea of returning from the dead in whatever form that excites the human imagination—and if science can add an extra "edge" to such a notion, then so much the better. It has already been noted how William Godwin's (and Mary Shelley's) physician, Dr. Henry Cline, "resurrected" a sailor who had lain in a coma for some months and was to all intents and purposes dead. Such occurrences, while slightly infrequent, were not by any means uncommon. In an age when medicine was still finding its direction, patients were quite often revived from swoons and fits and went on to live normal lives. Sometimes, such "revivification" was done by medical men or even by scientists, and those so revived were treated with awe. Therefore, a creation of a living being from the remains of the dead may not have been all that far removed from human aspiration. And as religion assumed less of a central role in the idea of bringing life back from beyond the grave (after all it, was Jesus and the prophets who brought the deceased back to life in the raising of Lazarus) and science came more and more to the fore, the perception that life could be created in the remnants of the dead might not have seemed all that impossible. The time in which Mary Shelley was writing was, after all, a new age in which many things seemed possible. That ideal has stayed with us throughout the years, even though the initial ideas of Giovanni Aldini, galvanism, and the legends concerning Johann Dippel have passed into history. The shadow of Frankenstein, that huge and lumbering monstrosity as portrayed in James Whale's film, seems to stretch across the centuries and into our own time.

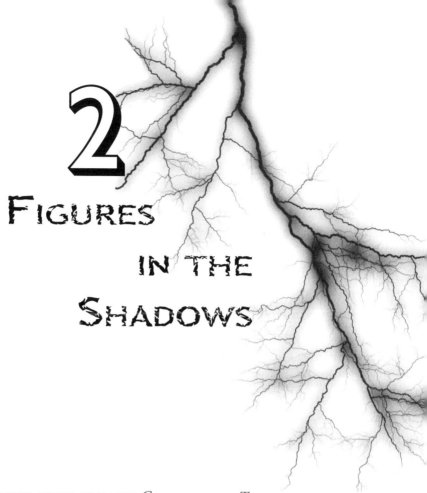

2
FIGURES
IN THE
SHADOWS

LET HIM WHO WOULD FORM THE GOLEM DO THIS. TAKE VIRGIN SOIL FROM A PLACE WHERE NO MAN HAS DUG. THE SOIL SHALL BE KNEADED WITH PURE SPRING WATER TAKEN DIRECTLY FROM THE GROUND WHERE NO MAN HAS DRUNK. IF THIS WATER IS PLACED IN ANY VESSEL, IT MUST BE THAT OF PURE CLAY AND CAN BE NO LONGER USED. HE THAT MAKETH THE GOLEM MUST BE PURE OF THOUGHT WHILST DOING SO AND LIKEWISE BEFORE DOING SO. HE MUST WEAR VESTMENTS THAT ARE WHITE AND CLEAN AND PURE. HE MUST SAY THE WORDS THAT BRINGETH LIFE AND MUST MAKE NO MISTAKE OR ERROR WHEN HE SPEAKS, NOR IN THE PRONOUNCING. NO INTERRUPTION WHATSOEVER MAY OCCUR. THIS IS THE WORD OF THE RABBIS.

—INSTRUCTIONS FOR CREATING A GOLEM, TAKEN FROM THE 17TH-CENTURY WISDOM OF THE RABBIS AND FROM THE ANCIENT SEFER YETZIRAH

Sefer Yetzirah

Mankind, so we are told by many Creation stories—including those of the Christian and Jewish traditions—was formed from the dust of the earth or the mud at the bottom of a river or ocean. Our ancestors were made by a Supreme Creator who somehow brought the elements together, shaped them, and breathed existence into these lifeless vessels. In a sense humanity was the true child of dust and clay. But, as we have already noted, the creation of such beings was usually the prerogative of the Supreme Being (whatever Mankind perceived him or her to be) alone. What if *Mankind* could gather up dust and clay and shape them into beings into which life could then be breathed? If the gods could do it then, perhaps, others could too, and maybe just as well.

In classical Greek mythology—and in other mythologies as well—when men were first created from dust and clay, they were weak and insipid beings, barely able to stand upright. In some versions of the Creation story, the Greeks believed that they had been created by the Titan Prometheus, who had scooped mud into his hand and had molded humans. However, there seemed little difference between humankind and the animals, and if there was, it was to the detriment of the humans—men were largely shapeless and went about on all fours and appeared to have no great intelligence. And this was repeated in a number of other versions of Creation, for example in Babylonian tales. Among the ancient Semites, the Creator made several attempts at forming humans before He (or She) actually got it right. There are stories in ancient rabbinical lore of Adam Kadmon, the prototype human who was created shortly before Adam, the forefather of Mankind, but who was not as perfect as the Creator would have liked, and so he was discarded. In the legends concerning him, Adam Kadmon is described in various ways, sometimes as a recognizable man, but at other times as a lumbering hulk of partially formed mud or clay—a proto-man.

How, it was asked, was the Supreme Being able to create humans, even if partially formed? Was there a set of instructions which He or She followed into order to bring nonliving material into a vibrant, breathing existence? And if there was, might others not be able to do the same if they knew the Divine formula? These were the questions that concerned the thinkers among some of the early peoples, especially the Semites.

Indeed, the Semitic peoples held that it *might* be possible to create life from the dust of the earth or the mud of the river, just as God Himself had done. However, the way in which this was done was a great secret, and was not given to everyone. Only certain learned and extremely holy men might be able to do this, but even then it was not easily done. The person who desired to do it must be both pure and holy, and the process was as much about discipline and meditation as it was about the actual formation of the creation. In fact, the forming of the entity was in many ways of a secondary importance; it was the mystical thinking behind the act of creation and observance of strict traditions and formulae that were paramount. Therefore, the being that was created was not an idealized man (even the creation of an extremely holy man could not attain God's perfection), but a creature of perhaps limited intelligence and malformed shape. And above all, it was a being that physically showed its origins in the clay of the earth. It was a shambling, lumbering figure that kept mainly to the shadows. And, having little will of its own, it served to carry out the will of whomever had formed it.

Many of the early rabbis believed that it was possible for an exceptionally holy man to gain knowledge of the formulae and the words of power that Yahweh had used to form men out of the dust. Indeed, Yahweh had revealed this knowledge to certain early patriarchs—most notably Abraham—who had recorded it as secret text, known to very few. This text, originally attributed to Abraham, was then passed down and modified by a core of rabbinical scholars until it became codified in a formal text—the Sefer Yetzirah, or Book of Creation (or Formation). This belief came very much to the fore in Europe and the Middle East during the medieval period when such a text was presumed to be in circulation. Much of the codifying work, tradition stated, was done by the students of the Rabbi Yehudah (Judah) ha-Nasi (the Prince), also known as Rabeinn ha-Kadosh (Our Holy Rabbi), an influential Hebrew teacher who lived in Judea around the second century AD, at the time of the Roman occupation there. He and his students are credited with compiling one of the first *Mishnah*, which would form the basis of a large part of the Sefer Yetzirah. This was known as the Old Torah (or the Oral Torah), and was supposedly a distillation of ancient (and often secret) wisdoms, which had been passed down directly by the patriarch Abraham, following certain conversations with Yahweh. Another part of these debates would also, together with a body of text known as the *Gemara,* form the basis of the Talmud, the guidelines that informally influenced and governed early Jewish behavior and morals.

In a work known as the *Talmud Bavli* (or Babylonian Talmud) there is an intriguing legend that has resonated in our modern world. It tells of two of Yehudah ha-Nasi's disciples named Rabbi Hanina and Rabbi Hoshaiah, who, using the formulae and text of a prototype of the Sefer Yetzirah, created a three-month-old calf. This, of course, was well in advance of the cloning techniques of modern times, and is suggestive of some of the life creation, which had characterized more modern scientific thought. The calf was not perfect, of course, but similar to the more recent Dolly the Sheep it was weak and subject to disease. Thus, explained the text, only Yahweh could create the perfect creature.

The actual writing of the Sefer Yetzirah was controversial and provoked discussion among medieval Jewish scholars. Most rabbis, such as the venerable Yehuda Halevi (1075–1141) trace the text (with later minor amendments and some debate as to the actual meaning of words) directly to Abraham, who received it directly from Yahweh. However, others suggest that its source may have been the early Rabbi Akiba ben Youseff, a teacher of the Geonim.

The Geonim were a group of Tannaim scholars—mystical sages of the first century who considered the early Semitic oral traditions. They existed between the years 50 and 200 AD). It was believed that the scholar had received the formula in a mystical vision and had remembered it long enough to write it down. This formed the basis of the book of Creation, which the Geonim added to and refined. From this, the early patriarchs could create men, though not as perfect as those created by Yahweh. This tradition, which was first suggested by the mystical and Talmudic scholar of Safed in present-day northern Israel, Moses ben Jacob Cordova (1522–1574), in his book *Pardes Rimmonim* (first printed in 1591), is usually discounted, although, in the complicated world of early Jewish mysticism, some aspects for the creation of the Golem have been accredited to Rabbi Akiba.

This was the source of the Golem legend—the hulking figure formed out of clay that lumbered through Jewish mythology, doing the bidding of the holy men who had created it, with no real intelligence of its own. The word *Golem* means "shapeless or unformed" in ancient Hebrew and refers to the lack of actual human definition in the finished creature. In the Old Testament—Psalm 139:16—it mentions "my unshaped form," which translates in Yiddish into the word "goylem." In more modern Hebrew, the word can mean "rock," "fool," or even "dumb." In the early Mishnahs of the rabbis it could also refer to "an uncultured or ignorant person," and might be used as a term of abuse or as a patronizing description. In recent times the word has become a Yiddish insult relating to someone who is clumsy or slow. One of the characteristics of the Golem was its inability to speak; this was often taken as a lack of understanding or as a lack of intelligence. Its shapeless form was attributed to the mud or clay out of which it had been formed, and so we are left with the abiding image of a lumbering humanoid figure, which is apparently very much under external control. It appears, to all intents and purposes, very much like the zombie of Haitian and Caribbean folklore. In this respect it can be used as a slave and, having no will of its own, will unquestioningly carry out the orders of its creator/

master. All traditions agree that the Golem, being less than perfect, has no soul (only the Creator himself could bestow these upon his creations), and therefore cannot make a moral judgment, so it can, technically, be instructed to harm or even kill.

Creating the Golem

So how, according to Jewish lore, is the Golem created? In the earliest stories concerning this act, the creature is created merely by shaping a figure of clay mud, roughly approximating human form, and then speaking a certain word or incantation over it. This word or formula is said to have been given directly to Abraham by Yahweh, and was passed down through the years in an oral fashion. However, this tradition is sometimes disputed. Some sources (for example, the Egyptian mystic and teacher Sa'adiah ben Yosef Gaon, AD 882–942) say that the patriarch copied the Words of Power onto a bark scroll, which was then passed down and used among the various holy men; this would form the central part of later medieval texts. Some rabbis have said that it was one word either spoken, written on the forehead of the clay image, or inscribed on a piece of paper placed on the figure's arm. It is traditionally held in many quarters that the word to bring the Golem to life was *emet*, meaning "truth," which was to be written in the mud or clay above its eyes. If the creator (or anyone else) desired to destroy the creature then all they had to do was remove the first aleph to make the word *met*, meaning "dead" or "inert," which would reduce the Golem to mud or dust once more.

The original form, shaped from the mud of the earth, might be very small, for once it had been activated, the Golem would grow to man-size and sometimes beyond, depending on the arrogance of its creator. Perhaps this later belief was added to ensure that only humble and penitent men would create such a creature. There is a story about a particularly vain rabbi named Elias (thought to have been Rabbi Elijah ben Shem of Chelm who

died in 1583) who sought to make himself famous and show how holy he was by creating a Golem. He created the clay image and placed the Word of Power on its forehead. The Golem began to grow and Elias spoke the formula that would restrict its size to a manageable human form. However, in his great arrogance, he made a mistake and the creature continued to grow unhindered. It grew until it was a giant and Elias could not reach the word on its forehead to remove the aleph and destroy it. However, he asked the Golem to remove his shoes, and the being had to kneel down to do so. This allowed the rabbi to remove the aleph and so return it to its natural unformed state. However, there was now so much clay that it fell upon the holy man and crushed him to death. The story was widely told as a warning to all prideful people who would seek to create the monster for their own ends.

Although the use of the word *emet* written on the clay forehead was generally accepted as the early ways of creating a Golem, as usual there was some debate on the matter and other ways were also suggested. Some early scholars argued that it was not the actual *utterance* of the word that created life (though the intonation and phrasing were extremely important); it was the way in which the word was *written* that activated the Golem. Thus, great attention had to be given to the actual formation of words and characters when writing out the incantation. Among those who took this view was supposedly the venerable sage Shimon bar Yohai (or Yochai), who lived around AD 70 and was one of the Tannaim. He was also a follower and student of Rabbi Akiba ben Yosef, and he argued that it was the *direction* and *positioning* of the written characters that was important in the creation of life. Properly directed written characters, correctly placed, together with the proper intonation of the Words of Power were essential in the creation of a Golem.

This belief also stated that Adam Kadmon had been a Golem and Yahweh had only chosen to reveal the imperfect formula to Mankind so that no one could make perfect humans. That was the sole prerogative of Yahweh alone.

But it was possible for men to create the *semblance* of life, or so the learned rabbi said.

Shimon bar Yohai's opinions were fundamental to the understanding of the creation of life and of the creation of the Universe in general. As a scholar and hermit, he shut himself away in a cave for more than 13 years, studying and interpreting the Torah—the first five books of Moses. He was visited regularly by the spirit of the prophet Elijah—one of the great figures of Judaism—who instructed him in many things, including his understanding of the creation of life. Under the direction of the spirit, Rabbi Shimon set out much of this knowledge in one of Judaism's most mysterious books, the Zohar (Book of Splendor or Radiance), which is a treatise of mysticism and cosmology. It was written in a strange, exalted, and convoluted form of Aramaic, which reflected the often obscure concepts that were put forward. The Zohar became one of the fundamental books of the Jewish Kabbalah, a mystical way of thinking and writing. Although writings concerning the cosmology of the Universe (including those of Rabbi Shimon concerning the creation of life) were passed down secretly among the rabbis, the Zohar and attendant works were not formally published until medieval times. The Zohar was published in Spain in the 13th century by the Iberian sage and mystic Moses de Leon. And, as usual, there is also some dispute about the authenticity of this work. Nevertheless, such mystical tomes were central to what became known as the school of *Kabbalistic* thought. The Kabbalah was a system of mystical and esoteric thought, set out in teaching and writings that concerned itself with the explanation of the world and the cosmology of the Universe. It relied heavily on traditional Jewish literature and on certain secret books that had been reputedly passed down from the early times. It was what might be termed "hidden lore," and was often referred to in general terms as the Oral or Hidden Torah. Included in this secret knowledge was the creation of life as defined and amended in the Sefer Yetzirah and the written formula for creating a Golem.

As time passed, the instructions for the creation of the Golem became more and more complicated, as the rabbis refined, debated, and interpreted the early wisdom. For example, not only did the Words of Power have to be written and positioned correctly, but also the person who created the creature had to meditate and pray for a certain period beforehand. The would-be creators also had to abstain from sex, because their thinking had to be clear and pure and not distracted by worldly things.

A number of texts contradicted each other with regard to bringing the Golem to life. Most, however, agreed that a certain phrase or connecting powerful words must be used. These were not necessarily written on the Golem's forehead as *emet* had been, but might be inscribed on a piece of paper, which was then placed in the mouth of the image one desired to be animated. The removal of such a parchment would destroy the creature. In some variants of these instructions, the words had to be written in human blood, as only this would stir the Golem to life. In others the written words are to be the secret names of God and must be written on calfskin (made from a calf that has only recently been suckled).

Uses for the Golem

Once created, the Golem's powers were extremely limited. It had great strength but little else. It could not converse with its creator, nor could it think independently. It had to be instructed in specific details and its actions had to be defined. In many cases the rabbis simply used it for doing housework or menial chores. The 16th-century Jewish mage, Samuel the Pious (Judah ben Samuel of Regensburg—c. 1140–127) was said to have created a Golem who went with him on his travels and who carried his luggage and performed menial tasks at the behest of the rabbi. In this respect the Golems functioned in a very similar way to robots or automatons in some of the relatively recent science-fiction stories. But there were those who said that some of the rabbis used the Golem for more sinister purposes:

the murder of Christians. Although it was denied by Jewish authorities, it was widely believed during medieval times that Golems were created and sent out in certain areas in order to kill leading Christians or those who were not Jews at the behest of certain groups of rabbis. Usually such claims reflected tensions between Jews and Christians in places where there was often persecution on both sides. In this respect, the Golem became a kind of "bogeyman" among Christians, a palpable symbol of the perceived Jewish threat. In Christian circles it was widely believed that groups of rabbis simply created the creatures in order to intimidate or slaughter non-Jews who dwelt within certain cities or towns. Legends regarding such groups permeated Christian folklore and often served to spark off "reprisals" against Jews. For instance, the mysterious "Brotherhood of Zion"—an alleged group of Spanish medieval Jewish mystics dedicated to the eradication of non-Jewish faiths—were said to create Golems with the sole purpose of driving both Christians and Moors from the Iberian Peninsula. There is no real evidence that such a grouping existed, but the tale may have been justification for the widespread massacre of Sephardic Jews in the Spanish city of Toledo in 1212 by Christian Crusaders following the Battle of Las Navas de Talosa against the Moors. However, rumors of secret Jewish societies, in which the Golem was used for malignant purposes, continued all through the Middle Ages and into later periods.

Of course the idea of the Golem was a two-edged sword: As well as supposedly attacking Christians for malign purposes, the Golem could also be used to protect Jewish communities from Christian attacks in periods of inter-religious tension. This is the source of one of the most famous stories concerning the creature: the Golem of Prague.

The Golem of Prague

In the traditional legend, the Golem's creator was said to be Rabbi Judah Loew ben Bezalel (c. 1520–1609), the Maharal of Prague. The term

Maharal is said to be an acronym of the Hebrew *Moreinn ha-Rav Loew,* which translates as "Our teacher Rabbi Loew." The nickname seems to have become a kind of title, which Rabbi Judah chose for himself and by which he was known. He became Rabbi of Prague in 1588 and was widely loved and respected. Also referred to as the "Exalted One," the rabbi was clearly one of the leaders and teachers among the Jews of Prague and was widely considered to be an extremely holy man. He was also considered to have great knowledge, particularly of the Kabbalah. Although he did not study the Kabbalah openly, he was widely respected as a Talmudic scholar, and it was said that he certainly studied mystical ways and the Oral Torah in secret and that he was quite learned in that respect.

It was a time of great tension between Jews and Christians. Jewish persecutions in some of the major cities were actively encouraged by the Christian authorities, who spread rumors that the Jews were kidnapping Christian children in order to kill them and use their blood in their Passover rituals. Such stories were particularly widespread in the city of Prague, and one of the leading Christians who encouraged them and who urged his followers to take up arms against the Jews was Rudolf II, King of Bohemia (1575–1608/11) and Holy Roman Emperor (1576–1612). Rudolf seems to have been a very complex man—a great patron of the arts, but an ineffectual ruler. He was a pious Christian and yet deeply interested in the occult (he studied both astrology and alchemy), which allowed for the development of a number of scientific advances during his reign. He unquestioningly believed the stories that Jews were abducting and murdering children and proclaimed retaliation against all Jews in Prague. The Maharal attempted to dissuade him, but the persecutions began. In anger, Rabbi Loew returned to the synagogue and planned to create a Golem that would serve as a Jewish protector in the city.

In order to do this, he had the help of several assistants, all of whom were sworn to secrecy on pain of death, regarding the Maharal's exact process of bringing the image to life. They gathered mud from the banks of the

Vltava River and fashioned a humanoid figure about the size of a man over which the Maharal performed certain mystical rites. In some variants of the tale not only did Rabbi Loew bring the Golem to life, but he also gave it a deerskin necklace that was emblazoned with several mystic signs that had been copied from one of the books of the Kabbalah. While it wore this necklace, the Golem remained invisible to the human eye. The creature was kept in the upper part of the Old New Synagogue in Prague. This place of worship was built in 1270 on the site of an already existing synagogue and incorporated elements of the older building into its structure. When the original synagogue was destroyed, the new house of worship became the old one. The Golem was supposedly kept in a room like an animal. For a time, the Golem worked as a protector, keeping the houses of the Jewish Quarter of Prague safe from marauding Christian bands. For most of that time, it remained under the control of the Maharal himself and behaved relatively well. Then something happened. The Golem seems to have developed thoughts and desires of its own and was becoming uncontrollable. It started to venture invisibly into Christian areas and to murder Christians as they went about their business. The Maharal was gradually losing control over it, and it developed a distinct and vicious personality of its own. It is here that the tale breaks into a number of variants.

In one variant, Rudolf II relented and called off the Christian persecution of Jews, pleading with Rabbi to call off the Golem. This the Rabbi managed to do before the creature became too powerful and too uncontrollable. He did this in one of two ways (depending on which variant of the story is told). In one, he managed to remove the aleph from the word *emet* in the Golem's forehead; in the other he removed a clay tablet (known to the rabbis as a *Shem-Hamforesh*) on which he had written the secret Words of Power in his own blood, from its mouth. However, in another version of the tale, the Maharal was unable to control the Golem, but was still able to summon it to face him. He did so and the Golem appeared at the Old New Synagogue, just as Psalm 92 was being sung. The Rabbi confronted the being, and by several tricks and stratagems forced it to open its mouth, from which he extracted the clay tablet. However, by now the Golem was so far advanced that it did not return to clay and dust, but lay inert, fully formed, like a statue. Rabbi Loew had it brought into the synagogue and carried to an attic geniza (a storage room designed for storing holy manuscripts and documents because it was believed that no text bearing the name of God should be destroyed) where it is still said to lie today. The Maharal subsequently forbade anyone from entering the geniza lest they should deliberately or inadvertently arouse the Golem.

The event is said to have imprinted itself on Jewish consciousness in Prague, and to this day it is said that the Old New Synagogue is the only place of Jewish worship in the world where Psalm 92 is regularly sung twice in order to commemorate the confrontation between Rabbi Leow and the Golem.

A number of stories were later told concerning the creature. One is that Rabbi Loew's son entered the geniza and used the clay tablet to reactivate the Golem, and so it is still active today; more modern stories have therefore grown up around it. It is said that in 1940 Nazi troops were burning Jewish synagogues in Prague, and some German soldiers entered the Old New Synagogue and, hearing the tales about the Golem, went immediately to the geniza, intent on finding it. They entered the attic, but were supposedly all torn to pieces by the marauding creature; of all the synagogues in Prague the Old New Synagogue was left untouched by German forces. This story is probably no more than a legend, but it serves to illustrate how the Golem story has been passed down to the present day. Recently, Czechoslovakian Chief Rabbi Karel Sidon stated that he receives hundreds of requests each year to visit the geniza of the Old New Synagogue in Prague in the hopes of seeing the Golem; unfortunately these are requests he politely but firmly turns down. He admits he has never been there, and it seems as if the Maharal's orders forbidding entrance are still being adhered to.

Of course, some stories say that the Golem is not there at all. In some versions of the Golem tale, Rabbi Loew's son, alarmed that such a violent creature should be kept within a synagogue, had it removed to the Zizkov area of Prague. Today Zizkov is a cadastral district (being delineated for the purposes of municipal taxation) of the city—it was once a separate town— and is considered to be extremely working-class. It was named after the formidable Hussite military leader Jan Zizka, and once enjoyed a reputation of being a very violent and crime-ridden sector. Why the Golem should be moved there is unknown. Other tales state that indeed the Nazis *did* find the Golem and that it was transported back to Berlin or somewhere else in Germany where it still lies, because no one actually knows how to activate it.

Rabbi Judah Loew was not the only influential rabbi that allegedly created a Golem or wrote extensively on the mystical background of the creature. One of the most celebrated Jewish mystical teachers was Isaac Luria (also known as Yitzhak ben Shlomo Ashkenazi, 1534–1572), who instructed a school of thought based in Safed in what was Ottoman Palestine. His teachings were broadly proclaimed to the wider world by his follower and disciple Hayyim ben Joseph Vital (1543–1620) and his son Shmuel. Luria's work was centered on the Zohar, but he gave the work fresh interpretations and claimed to have found new meanings regarding the cosmology that it contained. This, he stated, was an expansion on the work of the earlier rabbis, and moved the Zohar from simply a medieval text and into the early modern period. One of the major themes of Isaac Luria's work was the idea of *Shaar HaGilgulim*—the return of souls. Part of Luria's philosophy stated that those who had died before completing some important work were permitted to return in some form in order to carry out their unfinished obligations. The spirit suggested some of Luria's followers might be trapped in a clay figure and might be the animating force of the Golem. Intrigued by this notion, Luria is said to have created a Golem in order to test the theory. Using mystical techniques and incantations, he drew down the spirit of a dead man into a clay figure, but the result was so wild and uncontrollable that Isaac Luria had to destroy the figure and free the spirit. Later while considering his failure he suggested that instead of a returning soul he might have accidentally drawn down a *dybbuk* (a demon or an unclean spirit), which had given the Golem its life. Such things were drawn, it was theorized, to certain mystical characters or blood. This, in turn, led to speculation that some of the forces that animated the Golem might be evil or that some of the creatures might indeed be no more than the reanimated body of someone deceased, but by then Isaac Luria had turned his attention to other cosmological things.

The idea of the Golem—and particularly the Golem of Prague—has fascinated many people throughout the centuries and has found its way into mainstream literature and film. The 20th century in particular saw a kind of "rediscovery" of the creature and a marked rise in interest. Perhaps the most famous novel surrounding the being is Gustav Meyrink's *Der Golem*, which was published in 1914. The story was allegedly based on "an old Jewish folktale" and started out as a serial in the German periodical *Die Wiessen Blatter* between 1913 and 1914. It proved extremely popular and was eventually printed in book form in Leipzig in 1914.

The book has a disjointed feel—perhaps because it was originally published in serial form—but that only added to the intrinsic "mysticism" of the text, and it drew great attention from critics. Even though the Golem is rarely seen, its brooding presence dominates the book and the lives of the characters within it, such as the jeweler Althansius Pernath, the elderly Talmudic student Schemajah Hillel, and his daughter. In effect, the Golem becomes intertwined with the character of Prague itself, which is the dominant force within the tale. Although born in Vienna, Meyrink had lived in Prague for more than 20 years and knew the city well, so his work carries the ring of authenticity. He was also a student of both Jewish and Christian mysticism, and Kabbalistic hints and references litter his book. The story centered around the tale of the Golem of Prague and was supposedly based on a popular printed story in a collection of Jewish folktales, which had been printed in Germany by Judah Rosenburg, called "Nifla'ot Maharal im ha Golem" ("The Miraculous Deeds of Rabbi Loew with the Golem") in 1909. In fact, early drafts of *Der Golem* can be traced back to this time. The book is often seen as Meyrink's masterpiece and was hugely popular at the time, even outselling his later acclaimed mystical novel *The Green Face*, which was published in 1916.

The Golem on Film

The story also had an influence on the developing German film industry. Director Paul Wegener is thought to have been inspired by Meyrink's tale—and also the folkloric account of Rabbi Judah Loew—and in 1915, together with actor Henrich Galeen, released a silent horror film with the title *Der Golem.* In this an antique dealer (played by Galeen) created a Golem from an ancient rabbinical text, which seemed to come from Prague, with the intention of making it his servant. However, the Golem fell in love with the dealer's wife (thus implying that the Golem may have had human emotions), and when she rejected its advances, it went on the rampage, killing and destroying. The story was written by both Wegener and Galeen but was clearly based on the Prague legend of Rabbi Loew. The film was hugely popular in Germany and eventually found its way to America where it appeared in the early cinemas entitled *The Monster of Fate.*

The idea of the Golem so interested Wegener that he scripted (again together with Galeen) two more Golem films—*The Golem and the Dancing Girl* (1917), which was a comedy, and later *The Golem, How He Came Into the World* (1920). The latter once again used the tale of the Golem of Prague as its model. In the film a rabbi (clearly based on Rabbi Loew) creates a monstrous Golem with the intention of protecting his people. The creature grows too big and too strong and rapidly gets out of control, running amok and killing everyone, even those it is supposed to protect.

It sets buildings ablaze and destroys property, and the rabbi cannot control it. Finally, it is defeated by a little girl who removes a mystic amulet in the shape of a star (reminiscent of the Star of David) from around its neck. Although these films were much acclaimed at the time, they are now counted as "lost" with only fragments of *Der Golem* surviving.

However, in 1936, a French film *Le Golem* appeared in a number of Continental cinemas, which was clearly an homage to Wegener's work. This was directed by Julien Duvivier, and was based on the legend of Rabbi Loew. Once again, a learned rabbi makes a figure of clay which he brings to life with the intent of protecting his persecuted congregation. And once more, the Golem seems to develop a life of its own and runs amok. The rabbi finally brings it under control and destroys it, but not before it has killed and created much destruction. The Golem was now being seen as something of a destructive monster, and as something that could not be easily controlled, even by the most holy of men.

The Golem in Writing

The theme of the Golem was later taken up again by one of the more celebrated Jewish writers, Isaac Bashevis Singer (1902–1991) in a novel of the same name, written in 1969. Born into a strict Jewish family in Warsaw, Poland, which was then part of the Russian Empire, Singer was familiar with Jewish myth and legend, and hints of mythology and witchcraft are to be found in many aspects of his work. *The Golem* deals with the traditional motifs of the Golem story (Jewish persecution and the construction of a "protector"), and also explores superstition, gullibility, and the moral struggle between good and evil (the rabbi who creates the Golem begins to use it for some less-than-worthy purposes, leading to its development of an independent consciousness). The tale was originally written in Yiddish (then considered to be something of a dead language), only being translated into English in 1982. It was initially intended as a book for children, although many of Singer's "children's books" frequently have much deeper meanings for adults. His depictions of Jewish life and considerations of Jewish thought won him the Nobel Prize for Literature in 1978 and the title of a literary giant.

Throughout the years, the Golem continued to make sporadic appearances in both literature and film without ever achieving the status of the vampire, werewolf, or even Frankenstein. During those years many additional features were added to the Golem lore. For example, the legend of the Golem was limited with zombie lore from the Caribbean; it was said that salt, or a mixture of salt and human urine, was anathema to a Golem, and would drive the creature away. Similarly, echoing the Wegener film, it was said that an iron star, made in a certain way and inscribed with certain mystical symbols, would protect the wearer against the being and would render the wearer invisible. It was also said that the Golem had to return to some secret place during the hours of daylight where it could not be seen. Many of these ideas have really no basis in Jewish folklore, but add to the myth and menace of the creature.

And the man-made being seems to have briefly drifted into the realm of science fiction with its appearance in comic books during the early 1970s. *It, The Living Colossus* was one of the titles that the Marvel Comics Group launched in 1970 (*Tales of Suspense #14*), which features a great clay-like figure described as "a living statue." This had been activated by an alien race, but was sometimes under the control of Dr. Aloysius Vault who sought to use it for evil purposes. The title was not a success and was discontinued around 1972. It had, however, moved the idea of the Golem into the field of mainstream comic-book fiction and had brought the monster to a slightly wider audience.

And the idea of the living "man of clay" has persisted well into the 20th century. A story from Czechoslovakia, which was reported by the international press (most notably the magazine *Point of View*) in 1974 recounts how an engineer who lived on the Zlata Ulicka in Prague was found dead under the debris of a statue made from red clay. A policeman who had witnessed the event told reporters how he had seen a figure disintegrate before his very eyes into a shapeless mass (after presumably killing the engineer). Neighbors in the Zlata Ulicka became very excited at the report and stated that this was indeed the Golem, which still haunted the street and was sometimes seen after hours of darkness walking toward the area of Hradcany. Its sighting usually signalled a major disaster that affected the city, such as the May Uprising of 1968.

Although not one of the truly "classic monsters," the Golem lies somewhere at the back of the human mind, like a monstrous and lurking shadow, ready to emerge and threaten humanity. And even though it has emerged from time to time in story, legend, and film, perhaps it is not to be discounted and deserves much more of our attention.

The Mommet

The Golem frequently appears as a humanoid figure made from clay and brought to life by mystical or magical means, but it is not the only such man-made creature. Nor is it the only such being to have formed the stuff of nightmares. The Mommet, a man-made, animated creature made from wood, straw, and cloth has also terrorized a different part of the world.

In Somerset in England, the word *Mommet* is an old name for scarecrow (in Devon it is called a *Murmet*; in Bershire a *Hodmdod*, and in Wales a *Bwbach*), and this gives us a clue as to the type of man-made creature this was. As with the Golem, the Mommet could only be made by a Conjurer—a man or woman with sufficient magical skills to bring a creation to life—and the being had to follow an exact physical pattern, which was laid out on the ground before life was breathed into it. The ritual had to be performed in secret, usually under cover of darkness, and perhaps only at certain times of the year. The creature had to be built around a framework of wood, cut from a special tree or bush, although there is no firm direction as to what sort of wood this should be (the type varies from place to place). Straw and

cloth are also used to build up the body, and then a secret invocation, perhaps to very old gods, is uttered to bring this creation into living existence. As with the Golem, the Mommet seemed to have very limited intelligence, and so it depended upon its creator to guide it. In some instances, however, it was believed that the creature actually *contained* the spirit of the creator, which had been magically transferred into its body and thus directed it. In this version, the actual body of the creator sat in a kind of trance while the Mommet roamed about. However, this belief suggested more about the magical transfer of souls and, while significant, it does not seem to have been particularly widespread. In most stories, the Mommet seems to have been a lumbering Golem-like figure that followed directions from afar.

So how was the Mommet activated? Like the Golem it was through a Word (or Words) of Power, which were either spoken or written down and placed somewhere about its person. It could only be deactivated by speaking another Word or by removing the written words from his clothing (the piece of paper containing the Words was sometimes pinned inside its coat or another garment). Such Words, it is often claimed, could only be spoken by a Conjurer, and were passed down by word of mouth throughout the centuries. In other versions it was said that the Words of Power were also known to ploughmen who worked the land and who would sometimes use the Mommet to do their work for them—particularly if that work was heavy and back breaking. The Mommet, it was said, possessed phenomenal strength and was a tireless worker. The Words of Power were known to groups of ploughmen—who constituted a secret magical society—and passed it down among their members and precluded outsiders from learning their secrets. This may well have been a society like the Horseman's Word in parts of Scotland (a secret society of people who worked with horses in which secret formulas for controlling the animals were passed down). However, perhaps like some of the alleged Freemason rites, the initiation rituals were kept extremely secret and were said to be terrifying). Among the secrets that were passed down from ploughman to ploughman may have been the Words of Power for activating and controlling the Mommet.

However, it was also said that local witches and wizards also had the same powers. Such powers were still known and whispered about, largely in rural areas, right up until the early part of the 20th century.

Of course, as with the story of Rabbi Loew and the Golem, there were stories of the Mommet's creators losing control of the creature. An old tale from Somerset runs thus:

There was, at one time, living near a village which they say was Templecombe, an old woman called Auntie Madgy whom they said had a great reputation of being a wise woman or witch. There weren't a thing that she couldn't do and so she became very lazy and wouldn't even tidy her house. Those that came to see her always commented on how dirty and untidy her house was, but she couldn't be bothered to clean it. Because she had great powers, she resolved to make herself a Mommet that would do the work for her. So at the full of the moon on May Eve, she commenced to make the creature. She took a shirt that had never been worn and a number of other secret things including the noose that had hanged a man—since the spirit of a dead man would bring life to the creature. These she assembled in the moon light and in the center of a churchyard, which is the place to raise such things. And when the time was right she said the words that her grandmother had taught her, for they are passed down only in certain families, and the Mommet rose up as though it were a living person; it moved and walked like a living creature. Aunt Madgie brought it home, but kept it secret, for such things are supposed to be connected with witchcraft in the minds of ordinary folks. Each night, however, she spoke the words and the Mommet rose up and cleaned the house and drew water from the well in the darkness and nobody saw it, for she lived well beyond the village. When the sun came up, it would lie down in a secret place in the cottage and not stir again until darkness lay over the land. But it is unwise to meddle in such things, as the Bible itself says. Auntie Madgie used the Mommet so often—almost every night—that it began to think thoughts of its own and began to heed her less and less. It began to rise during the daytime—at twilight when the sun was going down—and would wander from the cottage; there wasn't a thing that Auntie Madgie could do to stop it. There was a word that she had heard her father speak that was supposed to end all dangerous and witchy things, but she could not bring herself to say it, for the Mommet was her own creation and it was useful to her. She couldn't bring herself to destroy it. So instead she treated it like a child, but it was a dangerous and malicious child and it soon began to break into people's houses and steal the food that they had laid up in their pantries, and drink their wine, beer, and milk. And if someone should come upon it, it would attack them most severely. Many knew, of course, that it was a Momment and who had created it. They were in awe of such things and they went to Aunt Madgie and told her to destroy it, for there was no one else in the village that could do so. And so when the Mommet was out and about, she went down and faced it. When it came at her, she said the Word of Power that she'd learned from her father, though it broke her heart to do so. It was like destroying a child that she'd brought into the world. The Mommet fell away to dust in front of her with the old coat that she'd put on it blowing away in the wind. There was nothing left of it, but the old wooden frame that she'd built it upon and even that wood was blackened as if it had been in a fire. There was little left. But she had to do it, for it was the only way that she could protect her village. That's the way of it with a Mommet.

Man-Made Monsters

A very similar story, also set in England, comes from Norfolk and is set near the Norfolk Broads.

On the road to Aylmartin and near the Shrieking Pits there was a minister living at one time. Now when I say he was a minister, you might think that he was a man of God and very holy, but this was not the way *this* man was, for he was a black-hearted villain and given to ungodly ways. They say that he practiced dark magic when he thought that no one saw him and that he had created a mawkin [a Norfolk word for a Mommet] to do his bidding. The thing never came out until it was dark and then it dug the garden and planted potatoes under the full moon. And there is some say that it cooked him his dinner as well, even though it was only a thing that was made of straw and bits of old wood. There are some that say that he sent it out to do things against them that he didn't like when the mood was upon him. But the minister didn't live long after he'd created the mawkin—some old stories say that it drew all the good out of him to maintain itself, but maybe that's only an old story. He died, looking very old beyond his actual years.

Throughout the years, the notion of the Mommet has changed slightly in folklore. Moving away from the idea of the Golem-like figure made out of wood, straw, and cloth, it has now become something like a voodoo doll in the tradition of Caribbean folklore. In addition to this, local witches perform spells that affect the person whom the doll is meant to represent. The term "Mommet" can also be used to describe a mischievous child and is even sometimes used as a term of affection. A long way from the notion of the menacing Golem or scarecrow, it seems.

Sinister Scarecrows

And yet the idea of the walking, animated scarecrow hasn't gone away, but still haunts the popular mind. The idea of a huge man-like figure, created from rags, straw, and sticks prowling about the nightbound countryside with a sinister intent still has the power to fill us with dread, and of course this has been picked up by a number of horror writers and filmmakers. The idea of a sinister scarecrow figure was used to great effect, for example, by the writer Russell Thorndyke in his Dr. Syn novels, the first of which was written in 1915. The series was so popular that it continued until 1944 with the last book entitled *The Shadow of Dr. Syn*. The entire series is set in the Romney Marsh area of Southern England, where the local minister of the village of Dymchurch-under-the-Wall—intriguingly named Dr. Christopher Syn—is also the leader of a band of smugglers under the alias of the Scarecrow. In order to command both respect and fear among his followers, he dresses up as a massive walking scarecrow, which issues orders and aids his followers in evading capture by the authorities. The figure is described as one of terror that often instills fear into those who would seek to capture him. The idea of the animated scarecrow set against the bleak and eerie background of the marshes both appealed to and awed readers, and became a great success, which only grew as the years passed. So much so, that, in 1937, they were the basis for a film, entitled *Captain Clegg* (one of Syn's aliases) directed by Roy William Neill and starring George Arliss. This was later followed by a Hammer Films production in 1962, directed by Peter Graham-Scott, as well as a three-part Disney television series in 1963—*The Scarecrow of Romney Marsh*—which starred Patrick McGoohan (then famous as *Danger Man* in a popular television series) as it's hero. The idea of a great figure dressed in ragged clothes and with a sackcloth mask/face certainly had overtones of the Mommet, and was quite clearly designed to strike fear into the hearts of locals and also of readers and cinema-going audiences.

Nor were the Dr. Syn books and films the only ones to feature the walking scarecrow-like figure of the Mommet. The list is too extensive to detail save to mention a few such as William Wesley's 1988 horror movie *Scarecrow* and the French film director Emmanuel Itier's 2002 straight-to-video shocker of the same name. The man-made scarecrow figure, it seems, still retains much of its earlier powers to terrify even the most logical of minds.

The Question of Life

As with the Golem, questions were asked as to what sort of force animated the Mommet and creatures like it. In other words, exactly where did the life that animated these figures *come* from? For the early rabbis, and with regard to the Golem, the answer was that it was part of the force that Yahweh had used in order to create the Universe, and could really only be good for those who believed in the Mommet. The bringing to life of the inanimate matter was usually done by a local Conjurer or by a secret society (usually consisting of ploughmen), and what motivated the creature might be an evil spirit. Such people often drew their power and authority directly from the Devil himself. Could therefore that animating power be dark and evil?

The same question seems to have also occurred to Jewish mystics such as Isaac Luria when considering the Golem. He had suggested that the clay figure might be inhabited and animated by a dybbuk or unclean spirit. And it was thought that certain rabbis could in fact summon such demons just as readily as they could holy angels. Such an idea was not new among Semitic peoples, and in the Middle East it stretches back into pre-Islamic history. Indeed, Luria seems to suggest that such spirits might be summoned by an able magician and used to animate dead bodies very much in the way that lightning had animated the monster of Victor Frankenstein. This, too, was an older Middle Eastern idea. It was thought that a magician could summon up such powers in the form of tiny whirlwinds (which were usually the sign of hostile spirits) and reanimate corpses in order to carry out their will or to use them as servants. Such beings then took on a hideous life of their own and either continued to live with their masters or were driven out into the desert where they lurked away from human habitation, but were still a sinister and malevolent menace.

Figures in the Shadows

Kahins

At least that was what the *kahins* taught. These were the oracle-mongers of the pre-Islamic period of the Middle East—men who wandered between the towns and cities, prognosticating the future, teaching esoteric ideas, and performing acts of great mystery and magic for the inhabitants. The name *kahin* may be similar to the ancient Hebrew *kohan* meaning "priest" or "mystical holy man," and indeed that's what these wandering men might have been, for some were strongly connected with pre-Islamic shrines and made their prophetic pronouncements in a fit of ecstasy and sometimes in rhyme. In fact, they were often regarded as being somewhere between priests and sorcerers. They were supposed to deal with the spirits that inhabited the deserts and wastes and to know their ways. They were even supposed to be able to command spirits and to be able to trap them in containers and receptacles (witness the story of Aladdin, in which the spirit or *djinn* is trapped in a lamp), which might even be dead human bodies that were then animated and came under the control of the kahin. This was apparently done through Words of Power very much like the creation of the Golem. The creature that some of them created was the *ghuul* or *ghul*, from which we get the modern word *ghoul*.

Ghouls

In traditional folklore, the ghoul is a flesh-eating monster that dwells in the almost inaccessible desert, and which devours travelers passing through its area. However, this may be partly invention of a Frenchman, Antoine Galland (1646–1715), who translated the supposed Arabic epic *One Thousand and One Nights* into French (from which it was translated into English). The tales contain many references to the supernatural, including tales of djinn and ghouls. It has, for example, given us the story of Aladdin and of Sinbad the Sailor with all their marvels. However, it is not clear exactly how much of this is actual Arabic folklore. Although there is no doubt that

Galland traveled extensively in Syria and the Levant in the mid-17th century (partly at the behest of the French East India Company), and that he heard and recorded many of the local folktales and stories in the places that he passed through, there is also little doubt that he changed and modified them to suit Western tastes. It is even possible that he made some of them up, although they were probably based on scraps of local information that he'd learned. Therefore, the ghoul, as it appears in *One Thousand and One Nights* may be different from the pure folkloric aspect of the creature.

For the early Arabic peoples, life was equated with breath (*nafs*) or the wind. The question about animating anything—for example a dead body—therefore was to "draw down the breath" from beyond the material world. The djinn, or spirit creatures, were characterized by the wind and usually manifested themselves in tiny whirlwinds out in the desert. These eddies and gusts where what the kahin observed and tried to draw down into inanimate objects such as dead bodies, thus creating ghuuls. The invocation for drawing down a djinn was supposedly complicated, but in order to release it and deactivate the creature that it had possessed all one had to do was utter the words *Mato hatfa anfhi* and deliver a deep wound or cut to the possessed body, which would allow the spirit to escape like a breath of wind.

Muqarribun

Although the kahins were considered to be relatively powerful magicians, there were sorcerers who were thought to be even more powerful, and could draw down spirits with consummate ease. These were the *Muqarribun,* the Ghost Priests of Southern Jordan whose name translates roughly as "the Near Ones." These mysterious sorcerers were at one time associated with Wadi Rum, a strange rock formation that lies in the deserts to the east of the Jordanian city of Aqaba. The place is as mysterious as the Muqarribun themselves. It is said to have once been a city, originally built by the djinn, and is now the habitation of spirits that, at one time, the Maqarribun could control. It was said that the Ghost Priests could construct figures that the spirits would then inhabit, or else cause people to rise from their tombs, animated by djinn whom the sorcerers had called down from the Wadi—in many ways similar to the Golem. The motives of the Ghost Priests were always questionable and strongly hinted at dark sorcery.

The Muqarribun were also said to be the protectors of dubious knowledge, which had been passed down across the ages from the time of Creation. This was contained in a number of scrolls and books that contained Words of Power supposedly used in the creation of the Universe—what they referred to as "the whispers of angels"—which had the power to ignite the spark of life. These were texts such as the secret portions of the Katib al Amr Sihry and the so-called Books of the Angels, which partly formed the basis of their formidable magical reputation. Indeed, some of these alleged and dubious tomes held by the desert sorcerers are said to have formed the basis for the famed books that appear in the works of the American horror writer H.P. Lovecraft—particularly his *Necronomicon*. There is also the implied idea that the "mad Arab" Abdul Alhazred, who supposedly wrote *Al Azif* (the text on which the *Necronomicon* was allegedly based) may have been one of the kahin or may have had contact with the Ghost Priests at Wadi Rum (said to be the location of Iram of the Pillars).

When created by the Muqarribun, the ghuul might prove extremely vicious, but was still subject to the will of whomever had created it. The spirit or djinn that dwelt in it might be very hostile toward humans and this might be reflected in its behavior. Once it had fulfilled its purpose the creature was turned free into the desert wastes to fend for itself as best it could. This may well have been translated into the flesh-eating monster of Galland's sometime translations of old Arabic legends. Perhaps some of them *did* eat flesh and perhaps some of them were based on the wild desert hermits who sometimes may have resorted to cannibalism in order to survive in an inhospitable landscape. Yet though they dwelt in the wild, the Muqarribun were still supposed to retain some sort of control over them and might still be able to command them. A legend, said to be from Southern Jordan, runs thus:

There was a village on the edge of the desert, near a waterhole, that was plagued by a fearful ghoul who tormented the people there. At night it would come into the village when the moon was dark, breaking into their houses and eating what it could find, and even attacking people as they slept in their beds. They said it had an unholy appetite and would eat human flesh if it could. But many of those it came up against were protected by the Holy Qur'an and so were able to resist its foulness. Even so it was a great nuisance and created much torment and suffering. In the end the people could put up with its attentions no longer. The headman of the village walked across the burning desert sand to see a Muqarribun who lived in a cave deep within the desert fastness. He walked for three days and three nights without stopping and eventually reached the sorcerer's cave. The Murqarribun was sitting just inside the entrance. He was a thin man dressed from head to toe in black robes. Like others of his kind, he was veiled so that only his eyes showed—hard and cruel—and regarded the headman.

"Step into the cool of my cave and out of the noonday heat," he said. His voice was like a barking jackal out in the desert. "And tell me why you have walked for so long across the burning sand to see me." And yet, he spoke as if he knew what the other's business might be. The headman trembled, but did as the Muqarribun asked.

"There is a ghoul dwelling in the desert near my village," he said at last, though his voice was shaking. "Each night it causes misery and torment among my people. There are those who say that only one of your kind can send it away, and so I have walked many miles to see you and to ask for your help. They say you are a very wise man." He hoped that flattery would do the trick. The Muqarribun considered.

"You are correct in what you say for the ghoul it is indeed a creature that has been created by magic and only we know how to banish it," he said slowly. "Such beings can only be driven away by the words of angels and it is only the Muqarribun who know such words." He reached into the folds of his dark robes and brought out something that looked like a circular iron amulet upon which a single symbol or word had been deeply engraved. "When the ghoul next appears, show it this. It will know that the word has been forged by the hand of its creator and it must obey for only its own creator can dismiss it. When it has seen the word, then you must say, "Roh!" ["Go!"] and it will return to the dust out of which it was formed. Now leave and trouble me no further, for I have much to consider here." And he sank back into the shadows of the cave and was lost to view. The headman returned to his village, still very fearful.

The next night the ghoul returned, coming from the desert with the wind. The headman went out to face it in the dark, clutching at the iron amulet. As the creature drew close he raised the token that the Muqarribun had given him; the thing did not seem to pause, but kept coming forward. Then the moon shone on the iron and it saw the word that was engraved there and hesitated.

"Roh!" said the headman as the Muqarribun had instructed him to do. "Begone!" The ghoul reared up and bared its teeth. "It is the word of your creator that commands you!" And at that the thing could not remain in our world, but fell to the ground with its mouth open. And the unclean spirit passed out of it like the wind and was gone. The body itself fell to pieces and turned to dust, and it troubled the village no more. The amulet itself, though it was iron, became like brittle leaves in the headman's hand and it too blew away as dust. The torment, it seemed, was past. But everybody knew that the Muqarribun out in the desert had created it, for only he who has created them can dismiss such things. The ways of such sorcerers are always unfathomable, for they deal with the djinn and with fallen angels."

The Idea of the Ghoul

The Jordanian story illustrates the fundamental belief that only those who created the creature through the summoning of an unclean spirit can return it to the dust, either by personally uttering the Word of Power or having it inscribed upon an amulet. This suggestion is also linked to some of the stories from Hebrew legend concerning the Golem. The ghoul as a resurrected figure certainly haunted the thinking of the early Arabian scientists—so much so that the astronomers named a certain star in the heavens after it. The star Algol in the constellation of Perseus is named after the ghoul and is usually referred to as "the demon star." Arabic stargazers thought that the star resembled the eye of a watching ghoul and treated it with awe and reverence.

Although their alleged occult powers certainly transcended those of the kahin and the fugara (local Bedouin healers and shamans), the Muqarribun were not the only people who were supposed to be able to create ghouls and such creatures out of the desert dust. The skill was also supposedly conferred on the mysterious Al-Saluba—the Lost Shamans of the Syrian Desert. These were a strange race of people who might have been Arabic and whom the Bedouin called Al-Saluban (meaning "crosses" as in "cross-breed"), or Al-Khlawiyah (from the Bedouin word *khala* meaning "wilderness," where they lived), and who may have been descended either from Greeks or from Indian peoples. It is not clear whether or not these people still exist, though they were said to be found in a stretch of desert between Palmyra and Mossul, and evidence of them has been found in some places like Kuwait as well. The only real major anthropological study of them was compiled by Lady Anne Blunt (the 15th Baroness of Wentworth, 1837– 1917), but local folklore credits them with formidable powers, including the power to create beings either from the desert dust or from the remnants of the dead. And yet nothing is truly known about these reclusive people, and they seem to have vanished from the pages of history—perhaps they have simply become merged with the Bedouin. They, too, contribute to the rich Arab tradition of creating the ghoul and other such artificial or resurrected beings

The idea of the ghoul also exercised a horrified fascination in Western minds. It continued to play a role in stories and stage plays, which certainly kept it to the fore of the popular imagination. In 1933, the British Gaumont Film Company released a movie bearing the title, based on a 1928 novel by Frank King. Although it did contain a number of supernatural and mystical elements, the story was more of a murder mystery in which the ghost or ghoul was revealed to be the twin brother of a deceased man, very much alive and certainly not a magical creation. The film did, however, feature an extremely celebrated cast including Boris Karloff and Cedric Hardwicke, both major stars of the horror genre. The film was released in the United States in 1934, and enjoyed something of a widespread success, largely as a murder movie.

More supernatural in tone was the 1975 offering from Tyburn Films in England (a short-lived British production company in the style of Hammer Films), once again entitled *The Ghoul*. Directed by Freddie Francis and scripted by Anthony Hinds, this also featured a celebrity cast that included Peter Cushing (then famous for his *Dracula* films), Veronica Carlson, and John Hurt. Set in the 1920s this followed the adventures of a group of socialites who take part in a road race, but due to a series of accidents they get stranded on a country estate in Cornwall owned by a mad and tortured former priest (played by Cushing) who has a sinister secret. His insane, cannibalistic adult son, the victim of some horrible plague in India where his father was a missionary, lives in the attic and gradually attacks them all in a welter of blood and gore. The film was released in America as *Night of the Ghoul* and was later re-released as *The Thing in the Attic,* and was a great success (largely because of its stellar cast). It was a last attempt to revive the Gothic film genre, which was so popular during the 1960s; however, it failed. Since then, the ghoul has become something of an ancillary figure in the horror genre, but perhaps it is no less terrifying for that.

The idea of the artificial servant created by mystic knowledge has formed a significant part of much of our folklore throughout the years. Whether it be the Golem, the Mommet, or the ghoul, the idea of a shambling figure created out of clay, rags, sticks, or even dead flesh still holds the power to terrify us. Many of these "terrors" originated among the Semite peoples in the area, which we now refer to as the Middle East. And this area may also have germinated the seeds of other later monstrous beliefs. It is to these that we now turn our attention.

3

THE THING IN THE JAR

IT SAID 'LET US MAKE MAN'—AND THUS MAN WAS MADE.

—ELIPHAS LEVI, *THE HISTORY OF MAGIC*

ACCORDING TO CARL JUNG, the first mention of the homunculus—the specially made "little human" of alchemic lore—appeared in the writings of an early Greek Christian mystic, Zosimos of Panopolis. Zosimos lived around AD 300 and belonged to the Gnostics, who took their name from the Greek word for "knowledge." In their complex theology, God was remote and unknowable, and had not created the world that we see around us. This had been created by an inferior deity called a demiurge (the word in Greek meant "public craftsman"), who was usually viewed as being inherently evil. Thus, its creations were also imperfect and corrupt, although there might have been a form of salvation for them. Such salvation came about through knowledge, which drew men closer to the Supreme Creator and meant that they were eventually reconciled with him/her. Included in this belief was a perception that humans were far less than perfect (they had been created by a flawed and evil entity), but also that they, too, might create life if they so chose.

This was the underlying theme of a series of texts that Zosimos produced, detailing some "dreams" that he had experienced. These are usually referred to as the "Visions of Zosimos." It is within one of these "dreams" that the homunculus appears, although as Jung is quick to point out, it is not referred to by that name. Instead, Zosimos refers to it as the *anthroparion*—a being not unlike a Golem, but certainly possessing more intelligence and guile. This being undergoes some sort of chemical change, which also involves self-mutilation and self-destruction, to be reborn again as another entity. Throughout his "visions" Zosimos encounters another such anthroparion—a Brazen Man, a creature made of lead—which continually destroys and redefines itself. Of course, Jung interprets the "visions" in a psychoanalytic style, but it is also clear that Zosimos was seeking to explain (in very visual terms) the processes of a new idea which had arisen in the Middle East, and which that later advance into Western Europe—the early proto-science of alchemy.

Alchemy

Although today we tend to view the work of the early alchemists simply as the search to turn base metals into gold or for the legendary Philosopher's Stone (which could perform a number of magical tasks and which has been recently placed back in the public eye by the Harry Potter books and films), alchemy was often a much more complex activity. It encompassed a whole range of discrete disciplines including dye production, assaying, medicine, matter theory, spiritual contemplation, and ideas regarding the creation of

life. The ancient alchemists were, therefore, chemists, metallurgists, and philosophers, and this invariably bled into their writings, theories, and experimentation.

Much of early alchemical theory concerned itself with the transmutation of natural elements into other forms that provided the basis of life. This followed an Aristotelian view that the basic elements—fire, earth, water, and air—might be interchangeable, and that such exchange might provide a life spark. The Greek philosopher Aristotle (384–322 BC) argued that the entire world and everything in it—including human beings—was composed of exactly the same substance (*materia prima*) and so life could in theory be created from inert matter through skillfull, and intelligent manipulation. Through boiling, it was argued, water could be converted into "air" (steam) and by cooling returned to water again. If it was frozen it became solid (ice), thus confirming the idea. And if this were true, then there was no limit as to what might be achieved by such transmutations. Life might therefore be created, this line of thinking suggested, in a vat, bowl, or container, and indeed a living creature might be "grown" from a seed, like a plant. The principles were in fact the same for the development of all things. It even allowed for the possibility that a type of life might be created from otherwise "dead" materials, such as stone, clay, or rock. This view would continue long into the Middle Ages in Europe and would indeed form the basis of much later Western alchemical experimentation.

Much of the early alchemical thinking, then, emerged out of philosophy and mysticism regarding the nature of things around the world—whether it could be changed or whether new pieces could be added to it. This early consideration had a lot to do with the origins of things and how they had come about. Part of the early philosophies were influenced by Greek, Semite, and Egyptian forms of thought about the nature of the Supreme Creator (assuming that there was one—although most schools of thought agreed that there was) and how he/she had brought the Universe into being. And similar to early Jewish mysticism, much of the tradition centered on esoteric debate and discussion among varying schools of thought and with very little practical information. A great deal of this speculation focused on religion, the exact nature of things, and the origins of the Universe and the creation of life within it, and was extremely mystical in tone.

Perhaps one of the first written texts that laid the foundation for alchemical experimentation appeared around the third century BC. It was entitled *Physika Kai Mystica* and was attributed to the Greek philosopher, mathematician, and writer Democritis (460–370 BC), although the actual author is more likely to be his disciple Bolus of Mendes (although some historians have suggested that the two men were actually the same person). The book was a mixture of mystical theorizing and directions for "multiplying" metals and elements such as gold, silver, and copper, as well as the "generation" of new elements in physical form. However, it was couched in the philosophical and difficult language that would become the hallmark of later alchemical writings and is therefore extremely awkward to interpret. The first practical alchemical text seems to have appeared somewhere around 250 BC in the works of Maria the Jewess.

Although she is often regarded as the mother of alchemy (and subsequently of early science), very little is known about Maria. Indeed she has passed into folklore as the sister of Moses—Miriam—or even with Mary Magdalene, the Mother of Jesus. She is thought to have lived somewhere between the first and third centuries AD and is mentioned by Zosimos of Panopolis in his writings. She is also referred to in the "magical texts" of the pseudo-author Ostanes (a name which may have been used by a number of "foreign" writers in the Greek Classical tradition to denote great wisdom) as being "the daughter of the King of Saba." (This, of course, is the kingdom in present-day Yemen that flourished from the eighth century BC to the third century AD, and is not to be confused with the present-day island in he Dutch Antilles.) Most of her work was centered on the construction of alchemical equipment and processes, such as the workings of furnaces and stills. Included among this is a sealed container in which life might be created, which, according to the early texts, is a significant tool for the alchemist. However, no real instructions seem to have been given for the creation of such life, although the suggestion of it was certainly there.

Ancient Texts

During the classical period when Greece and Rome ruled the Mediterranean a set of other texts began to emerge. Both their origin and authorship are uncertain, but other clay tablets that have been subsequently discovered attribute them to a god, although which god is also questionable. These are the writings of Hermes Trismegistus (Hermes the Thrice Great, in Greek), and they are a collection of seemingly magical papyri and dialogues. It is unclear whether the name referred to the Greek god Hermes (the messenger of the gods) or whether the scrolls originated in Egypt and the god involved was actually Thoth (who led the way to the Afterlife). The two gods, however, were worshipped simultaneously in a temple in the Greek-held Egyptian city of Khemnu, which the Greeks called Hermopolis. Both gods presided over writing and reading, and were often regarded as "civilizing deities"; the writer of the text is said to have been the real founder of scientific thought. However, there were many disputes about who actually had written the texts (it was generally accepted that it was a god—but which god?) and the meaning of the term "thrice great," which had attached itself to the writing.

Most Greek and Roman scholars did not think that the Hermes referred to was the Hermes of classical lore and discounted the writer of the text to the status of a minor god, if a god at all. The poet Cicero, for example, speaks of a Hermes (the fifth), a man-god who was worshipped by the people of Pheneus (Arcady) in southern Greece. He seems to have been a localized deity who was nevertheless credited with the slaying of Argus of the Hundred Eyes, the ever-watchful servant of the goddess Hera. To avoid the wrath of the deity, he fled to Egypt where he taught the people reading, writing, and the sciences, and became known as Thetys, Tet, or Thoth. According to some Greek writers, it was this Hermes who brought culture and civilization to Egypt, together with a more Hellenistic aspect to Egyptian life. Just to confuse matters, however, Cicero also mentions "the fourth Mercurius" (Mercury being another name for Hermes), who was "a son of the Nile" and "whose name may not be spoken amongst the Egyptians." It may be possible that this "fourth Mercury (or Hermes)" was a local god or even a local king of Egyptian origin who had been elevated to godhood. It seems likely, however, that the scrolls were attributed to a duality of local deities, who became identified with the more formal Greek and Egyptian gods Hermes and Thoth—who were concerned with bringing a "civilizing influence" to the early world.

Hermeticism

Whatever their origin, a whole plethora of texts began to emerge from around the Egyptian area, most hinting at both Egyptian and Babylonian schools of thought. All of them were attributed to the mysterious Hermes Trismegistus. At a guess the majority of them emerged from local temples and were in all probability written by learned priests and sages. They largely concerned themselves with the summoning of spirits, but also the animation of statues and inanimate objects, as well as the generation of life. Two main texts in particular (which are actually collections of shorter texts) are worthy of mention—the *Corpus Hermeticum* and the *Ascepius* (or *Perfect Sermon*). These formed the basis of what were known as "hermetic writings" from the classical world: the *Corpus* being mainly in Greek (although also in Egyptian and Babylonian) and the later *Ascepius* in Latin (the original Greek having been lost)—and would form the basis of scientific, alchemical, and magical thought throughout the Western world. Contained in these works, it was said (albeit in codified form) were many secrets—the transmutation of metals into gold, the elixir of life, and the method for instilling and creating life from "base substances." Couched in mystical language the texts provided a varied collection of spells, philosophical thought, and questions on the nature of the Universe, which appear to have risen out of a number of traditions. The texts are seen as redactions or

edits of perhaps earlier works, which may have already been in circulation. The *Corpus* is important, as it undoubtedly provides a distillation
of Hellenistic thinking regarding the nature of the world from as early
as the second century AD and gives a glimpse of Mankind's first tentative
steps toward a more formalized science. The works of Hermes Trismegistus
would continue as a source of "hidden wisdom" all through the medieval
period and even into the 20th century through a number of secret societies that flourished during this period. And of course, Hermes Trismegistus
has bequeathed us an important scientific term, denoting in part his great
contribution to modern science. That term is *hermeticism,* which is derived
from his name and means "completely sealed." During the Middle Ages
it was one of the "buzz words" of the alchemists and usually referred to a
sealed vessel in which elements could be mixed and fermented, and perhaps
even life might be created. "Hermeticism" therefore almost became the description of the secret processes that the alchemists were said to carry out,
and symbolic of the secret knowledge that they were said to pass on, one to
another, thought the medieval period.

Geber

This "hidden wisdom" was of course not simply confined to the classical worlds of Greece and Rome. There were stirrings of the early alchemical sciences in the Middle East as well, as Arab thought and culture began
to take an interest in such things. And once again it was heavily tied in
with religion and the mysteries of life. One of the great religious thinkers
of the time was Ja'far al-Sadiq (c. 702–c. 765), a respected holy man and
teacher who had been born in the city of Medina, Saudi Arabia. He wrote
on a number of topics; his opinion was venerated as that of a great Imam
by those who followed him. One of these was the Arab scholar Abu Musa
Jabir ibn Hayyan, who is said to have lived between AD 721 and 815,

although others give slightly different dates. He would later become known as "Geber" in the West, and would be known as such in medieval Europe.

Jabir ibn Hayyan's contribution to the fields of medicine and developing scientific thought consists of more than 100 treatises, which included more than 22 on alchemy and chemistry. These included *The Book of Stones*, but more importantly the *Kitab al-Kymya* (or *Kimia*), which was translated in the West by Robert Chester in 1144. The text concerned itself with the transmutation of metals and has given us word *alchemy*. The *Kitab al-Sab'een*, which dealt more with medical matters, was translated by Gerald of Cremona around 1187. Similar to the works of Hermes Trismegistus, this codified what was called the *Ilm-ul-Jafr* (the Wisdom of Ja'far), which is actually a compilation of knowledge gleaned from numerous sources in what is now the Middle East. Once again, the language is excessively mystical and is tied to Islam (ibn Hayyan was an extremely religious man), and many of the scientific processes are couched in allegories and are therefore difficult to interpret, but, together with the works of Hermes Trismegistus, this corpus of texts would provide the basis for alchemy and scientific development in Europe. Among the myriad texts attributed to Jabir ibn Hayyan are the ingredients and elements for the production of life, and are said to be directions for the creation of a homunculus or "little man," and for the ignition of artificial life.

Takwin

Indeed, part of the quest of many Islamic alchemists (including Jabir ibn Hayyan) was the concept of *takwin*. In the Arab world, this referred to the creation of artificial life within a laboratory or alchemical chamber. It was viewed by many as an emulation of the act of Creation, similar to what is detailed in the "secret wisdom" of the Hebrew Kabbalah; the life that was created was both plant and animal—including the generation of humanoid life such as a homunculus. And, like the early Hebrew and Hellenistic texts, the creation of such life was bound up with religion and mysticism.

The Thing in the Jar

For example, when Jabir ibn Hayyan writes about such creation, its meaning is clouded by heavy mystical terminology and obscure language, so the reader is not always able to tell whether he is speaking literally or metaphorically. "The Purpose," he writes in the *Book of Stones,* "is to baffle and lead into error everyone except whom Allah loves and provides for." This deliberately obscure language would later become a central feature of the mysteries of alchemical endeavor during the Middle Ages.

One of ibn Hayyan's pupils was said to have been Muhammad ibn Zakariya al-Razi, although the actual relationship between the two men is questionable. (Al-Razi is said to have lived between 865 and 925, by which time ibn Hayyan would have been dead. But all these dates are open to interpretation.) Al-Razi is said to have been born in Rayy, a Persian city that corresponds with a location near present-day Tehran in Iran. He may have actually started out as a musician, but switched his attention to alchemy and the study of medical science. He produced a number of works, including the *Kitab al-Asar* (*Book of Secrets*) with a supplemental treatise entitled *Sirr al-Asar* (*The Secret of Secrets*), which is probably his most famous work. Some of his many treatises have been translated into a variety of languages, including Latin, which made him accessible to medieval European alchemists—one of his treatises became one of the books bearing the title *Liber Experimentium* (a popular title for alchemical writings in the Middle Ages). Although a great majority of his works deal with medicine (he was one of the earliest medical writers, for example, to differentiate between measles and smallpox), some of his more esoteric works deal with *takwin,* or the creation of life. However, as with many of these early writers, the language used is so obscure that it is difficult to know whether he is speaking literally or metaphorically. However, he seems to suggest that with the right elements and conditions such a thing is both scientifically and medically possible. Although he may not have done it himself, he may have heard of Arab alchemists who have managed to do so, though the life that they created was far from perfect. Al-Razi went on to become the director of the main hospital in Baghdad during the reign of Caliph

Al-Muktafi (901–908) and at a high point of the Abbisid Caliphate, from where he continued to write mainly on medical matters. However, in some of his texts, he had laid the idea for the homunculus in the popular mind.

Alchemy in the Far East

Alchemy was also being practiced in the Far East, and this would have its own influence on Western thinking. Alchemial writing started to appear in China during the time of the First Emperor of the Ch'in Dynasty (AD 221–206)—a union which was forged when the warrior king Shih-huang unified the warring kingdoms and created the nucleus of China. These were redacted and codified by the sage Huan K'uan (73–49 BC) who linked them strongly to a developing Taoism. Many of these were concerned with the transmutation of metals and creating gold—in fact, some writers such as J.C. Cooper (1990) have argued that the making of "counterfeit gold" was so widespread around 150 BC that local authorities issued a series of laws against its manufacture and that alchemists attempted to make it on pain of death (whether this is true or not is unclear). However, it is known that one of the early emperors around 60 BC had his own alchemist—a man known as Liu Hsaing, who was given the title of Master of the Recipes—working on a formula to vastly prolong (the emperor's) life.

Although a good portion of Chinese alchemy was directed toward transmutation of substances and creating potions that would immeasurably increase human lifespan—the so-called Golden Liquid that could be drunk like a medicine—there were also experiments carried out to see if life itself could be created. None appear to have been successful, although stories existed that beings and animals had been created in secret. A number of Chinese emperors viewed such tales with both suspicion and alarm, and passed laws against alchemy in general except that specifically sanctioned by the Royal household. This may have been because of rumors and stories that certain hostile warlords were employing alchemists to create ferocious and unthinking warriors, which could then be formed into armies to attack the emperor himself. None of them lived long, nor appear to have had any appreciable intelligence. Of course, these may just be rumors designed to unsettle the authorities in certain local areas.

Arguably the greatest of all the early Chinese alchemists was the venerable sage Tsou Yen, who lived during the third and fourth centuries BC. He was born in Shantung (Shandong) Province somewhere around 305 BC (although the exact date is questionable) and rapidly became one of the greatest scholars of his day. Tsou Yen is said to have written many treatises on philosophy and on alchemy (including certain texts concerning the creation of artificial life), although nothing survives and there is really no evidence that he actually wrote anything at all. It was he, however, who first put together the idea of the Five Elements Theory, which was central to Chinese alchemical philosophy. These were the elements of earth, fire, metal, water, and wood, which were the basic elements of worldly existence. They could be interchanged through the alchemical process and might be used to create new elements such as the basic spark of life. His teaching was widely accepted by the surrounding kingdoms and it is said that he became a kind of alchemical and scientific advisor to King Hui of Wei (370–319). It is at this king's summer palace that Tsou created some sort of tiny being for the monarch—a creature that both moved and spoke and showed at least a glimmering of intelligence. The being only survived for a short time before it expired and immediately turned to dust, but it is counted as an early form of a homunculus. The story is almost certainly false—according to some biographies of Tsou Yen's life, King Hui of Wei would have been long dead even before he was born, and thus he could not have served at the monarch's court as a form of scientist/magician. There is no doubt, however, that he was a venerable man and was extremely highly regarded. Legend says that another monarch—King Cho of Yen (311–278—served as his herald when he moved through the northern provinces, so high was his popular esteem. Certainly he is widely regarded as the father of Chinese alchemy, and is credited with setting the notion of creating artificial life.

Around the first and second centuries AD a set of texts began to appear in the West that reputedly had their source in China. A mixture of philosophical, alchemical, and early scientific theoretical works probably dating from around the sixth century, they were attributed to mysterious figure known as Laozi. The name simply means "Old Master," and it is unclear as to when this person (if indeed he was a person) actually lived. Some stories about him, for example, say he was in his mother's womb for 62 years and emerged as a fully grown sagacious man; in others he is consulted by Confucius on points of philosophy or by the Yellow Emperor (in Chinese mythology he is the forefather of all Han Chinese and he brought writing and other skills to China); in other tales, he is depicted as having abnormally long earlobes and is referred to as "Old Longears." In some cases, however, Laozi is simply referred to as a god, similar to Hermes Trismegistus in classical and Egyptian antiquity. Today it is widely thought that Laozi was not a single individual at all, but rather a number of writers—the styles of a number of the documents appear inconsistent with each other—whose works have been compiled and redacted by others. It is also thought that the text emerged out of what became known as the Hundred Schools of Thought in early China, which existed between the years 770 and 221 BC. In its latter stages it was an exceptionally bloody period in early Chinese history when various Chinese states made war on each other. Despite regional factionalism, it was a time of bureaucratic and intellectual expansion, which laid many of the foundations for the development of the country. Much of the thought that emanates from these texts is Taoist in tone (Laozi is widely believed to have formulated the Taoist philosophy in China) exploring Mankind's relationship with the natural world. However, a number of the texts credited to either Laozi or the Hundred Schools of Thought would appear to have been lost over time—references to them exist, but the actual texts do not.

Among them are said to be records of the creation of artificial life by Chinese alchemists. Although no details exist, some are said to have created both small animals and tiny humans in laboratory containers, growing them like plants from an alchemical seed. There were also supposedly instructions for the creation of metals—including gold—by organic means, and suggestions remarkably similar to those of Tsou Yen, which hinted that inert elements might be transmuted into some other form, including human flesh and life. However, as of yet there are no means of verifying that such texts did indeed exist.

Alchemy in Europe

All this "ancient knowledge"—classical, Middle Eastern, and Chinese, all passed down across the ages—formed a rich and heady mixture that began to coalesce and come to the fore in Western Europe during the early Middle Ages. From around the 12th century onward, alchemical work was taken up by alchemists working in places such as France, Germany, and England, who worked from ancient texts. But the great center for alchemical study was Spain, where it flourished at the time of the First Crusade in 1095. The alchemical ideals had been brought into the country by Moslem Moors coming there from North Africa and, initially at least, relied heavily on the Arabic texts. Their influence spread widely throughout the kingdoms of Spain, and throughout the next hundred or so years, the other influences of the ancient world began to slowly influence both alchemical theory and practice. In fact, it seems to have been in Spain that the word *alchemy* came into common currency (though it had been used before)—coming mainly from the Arabic word *al-kimia* meaning to transmute metals (although the original word had been the Greek *khemia,* which had the same meaning). Many of the Spanish nobility, who could afford copies of these texts, were probably involved in some sort of alchemical activity, and not even royalty was exempt from this.

Alfonso X, King of Castile (1221–1284, nicknamed "the Wise," because he is generally regarded as something of a scholar king) both tolerated and, it is said encouraged and dabbled in alchemy himself using texts that he had allegedly bought from Moorish merchants and from other sources. Indeed, around 1272, he is alleged to have written a major alchemical work entitled *Tesoro* (Treasure), and slightly later another treatise on the subject entitled *The Key to Wisdom*, both of which he claimed were edited translations of earlier Egyptian works. In some of these he discussed the possibility of creating life such as the homunculus through the fusion of elements—possibly based on the takwin of Islamic alchemical literature. This, of course, drew the disapproval of the Church, which decreed that God alone could create life. This was also a political move, because Alfonso was accused of "consorting with certain Moors" with whom he consulted on seemingly secret matters (probably regarding scientific matters). Fearing Islamic political inroads into Christian Spain, the Church clandestinely warned the monarch. Alfonso, however, had always turned a blind eye to such disapproval concerning his studies, so much so that when he had sought to become King of the Germans (which would also have named him as Holy Roman Emperor), the pope, Alexander IV, steadfastly opposed this, and he had to content himself with the title of King of Rome. Later, it is alleged that he received an informal rebuke from another pope, Urban IV (1261–64) concerning his "sorcerous" activities. And the pope's condemnation gives an indication as to how the Church viewed the activities of the alchemists—especially with regard to the transmutation of metals and the creation of life. Apparently this was something akin to witchcraft and possibly relied on the assistance of unclean and questionable powers. In 1317, Pope John XXII issued a Papal Decree—*Decrimine Falsi Titulus*—formally denouncing alchemical practice. The decree was aimed mainly at those who sought to transmute metals into what the papacy referred to as "false gold," but the pope took a broad swipe at all those who conducted such clandestine experimentation, no matter what its outcome. He expressly forbade the practice on pain of excommunication.

And yet, although the Papal Office denounced such practices, there were rumors and stories that several of the pontiffs had been secretly involved in alchemy. These stories may have been started by their enemies or by Protestant reformers (who viewed alchemy as the Devil's work, as did the Catholics), but the tales persisted and seemed to hint at all sorts of mysterious experimentation. The famous Pope Formosus (891–896), who became the focus of the terrifying Cadaver Synod, for example, was accused of practicing witchcraft, and creating strange potions, and creating small beings in jars or receptacles. Legend says that one of these resembled a frog with huge eyes, which manifested a "diabolical intelligence" and which "brought terror to all who saw it," although what became of this creature (and another that Formosus supposedly created) is unknown. The charge was, of course, a political one, trumped up by some of Formosus's political adversaries and enacted by one of his successors, Stephen VI. By this time Formosus was dead, but his body was exhumed, dressed in full pontifical robes, and placed on trial by Stephen, who is now adjudged to have been insane. It is possible that his alleged alchemical creations (if they actually existed) were destroyed upon his death.

Similarly, Pope Honorius III (1216–1227) was strongly accused (probably falsely) of both witchcraft and alchemy. He was accused of "having Moorish texts" about him, and of trying to find ways of turning base metals into gold and of seeking to create life in an alembic (sealed jar) within a secret room of the Lateran Chapel, in "defiance of God's order." All these beings were reputedly destroyed on the order of his successor Gregory IX. Though, this account rings false, because it was Honorius who oversaw much of the Fifth Crusade (1213–1227) against the Moors holding Jerusalem, and may be no more than a story to discredit his name. Even so, Honorious is still credited with the compilation of a grimoire, which is still extant, and also certain other alchemical writings, which have since been lost or allegedly destroyed on Gregory's orders.

And yet another pontiff who was said to dabble in magic and alchemy was the learned John XXI (1276–1277), the only Portuguese pope and the only physician who has ever succeeded to the Holy See. It was the interest in medicine, particularly ancient medicine that encouraged the pope to become involved in alchemy and, perhaps, in the creation of life. It is said that during the time that he served for the University of Paris (before becoming pope) he created a small man who later acted as a servant to him but who could not speak and had only limited intelligence. Incidentally, the same was said of Pope Anacletus II—the "Jewish Pope," who is now described as an "antipope"—who reigned between 1130 and 1138. Because of the pope's Jewish origins it was said that he had gained access to certain Hebrew manuscripts relating to the Golem and had fashioned a similar servant. Even John's bizarre death was said to be somehow linked to his alchemical practice. (He was crushed when a pile of books and part of the ceiling of a newly constructed library fell on him when he was supposedly asleep there.) There is no doubt that John was an extremely learned man and may well have been interested in the writings of alchemists, but there is no proper evidence that he was engaged in alchemical and occult experiments, which included the creation of life, as is sometimes claimed.

But if legend is to be believed, it seems that more than the popes were involved in alchemy and possibly in the development of artificial beings within the Church. From certain (admitted, questionable) records, it seems that some of the orders of monks might have also been involved.

The Templars

Foremost amongst such orders were the Templars. Formed in the Holy Land in 1119, just after the end of the First Crusade, by the French knight Huges de Paynes and his cousin Geoffrey Saint-Omer, this military monastic order was specifically brought into being to protect pilgrims on their way to the newly accessible Christian shrines. The Crusader King of Jerusalem, Baldwin II, granted the order the newly captured Al-Aqsa Mosque, part of the Temple Mount, as their headquarters. This temple was supposedly built on an even older one—said to be the Temple of Solomon. Although the order originally called itself The Poor Fellow Soldiers of Christ, they soon added "and of the Temple of Solomon" to their title. Buried in such a location were said to be a number of mystical and magical artifacts and documents, and the Order is supposed to have uncovered at least some of these. This gave them something of a mystical and even sinister reputation

among other orders, especially when the Templars began to rise in favor
with Church authorities, including the pope. Many of the stories about
them, therefore, may be no more than rumor spitefully circulated by other
orders of monks. But there is no doubt that the Templars did indeed advance
in ecclesiastical circles. Their protection of their rites and rituals, many of
which were held in secret, only added to suspicions about them. It was
rumored that the Templars had found certain scrolls in the ruins of Solomon's Temple, which were supposedly written by a legendary but mystical
figure named Melchezidek. Melchezidek had been the patriarch Abraham's teacher in Ur of the Chaldees. The Chaldees were said to be great
sorcerers and wonderworkers, and is mentioned early in Genesis 14:18–20;
however, he is described as the priest-king of Salem, which is an ancient
name for Jerusalem (Yeru-Salem). He was also supposedly born of a virgin,
who died during childbirth and was the sister-in-law of Noah. He was also
supposedly a survivor of the Great Flood. These texts had been pre-
served by Solomon, together with a sect of Hebrew priests, and contained
many mystical and alchemical formulae, including guidance on the creation of life. The Templar Order was later accused of creating homunculi
in several of its monastic houses across Europe during the 13th and early
14th centuries. Such creatures, it was said, were actually worshipped by the
order. There seems to be little evidence of this allegation that the Templars
practiced witchcraft. The order became heavily involved in finance—together with the protection of valuables of those who were on pilgrimage—
and initially began and developed one of the earliest forms of banking
in Europe. Many of the European monarchs were in debt to them—the
Templars may have covertly financed many of the European conflicts of the
time—and might have been glad to see the order collapse and their fiscal
obligations with it. However, the order enjoyed a great deal of papal patronage. In 1128, for example, Pope Honorius II granted them the right to
wear a white surcoat as a sign of their purity, and in 1147, Pope Eugenius
III granted them the right to forgive their own sins without reference to the
Vatican and to collect burial tithes on their own behalf. They always wore

the eight-pointed cross as a symbol of papal favor. Such favoritism only engendered jealously and mistrust in many of the other Orders who were not so favoured. Thus, the Templars acquired many enemies, both secular and from other orders who wished to see their downfall.

During the latter years of the 13th century, one of those monarchs who owed the Templars a great deal of money was Philip IV of France. As the French pope, Clement V (1305–1314), took the Chair of Peter, Philip saw his chance. Using his position as sovereign of France, he persuaded the pope that the Templars were practicing witchcraft and the dubious arts of alchemy upon which the papacy formally frowned. Clement was actually in a politically difficult position. His predecessor, Benedict XI, had died suddenly and poison was suspected—Clement was frightened for his own life. The Roman Vatican was a seething pit of conspiracies, as various families strove for papal power. He moved the seat of the papacy from Rome to Avignon—the beginning of what was to become known as "the Babylonian captivity of the Church"—and right into Philip's jurisdiction. The papacy was now dependant on the protection of the French king and Clement was more or less at his behest. In 1305, almost as soon as he came to the papal throne, Clement denounced the order, and in 1307, he moved against them with the support of a number of monarchs with Philip IV at the forefront. The Templars were arrested, Templar houses closed, and a number of the senior members of the order put on trial. Under duress from the medieval Holy Inquisition, a number of Templars did confess to horrible crimes against the Church and humanity, among them witchcraft and alchemy that included the creation of life using certain old scrolls that they had found in Jerusalem or under the direction of a dark god, Baphomet (thought to be a corruption of the Mohammed, the name of the Islamic Prophet). They had created such life to murder and steal on their behalf and to spy on God's servants so that they (the Templars) could move against them and increase their own wealth. As soon as the evil war was carried out, the creatures returned to dust, so that no trace of them could be found. These charges were trumped up and were little more than the outpourings of a fevered imagination (that of the Inquisitors), but they were readily believed in some quarters. It is not clear whether Clement believed them, because recently it has come to light that he secretly signed a paper—the Chinon Manuscript (signed at Chinon in France on August 17, 1308)—absolving the Templars and their Grand Master Jacques de Molay (the 23rd of that title), from all charges brought against them by the Inquisition. The Chinon Manuscript was stored away in the Vatican Secret Archives and was not discovered by scholars until late in the 20th century. It never came to light at any Templar trial, and de Molay, together with another senior Templar, Geoffroi de Chanay, were both burned at the stake as witches and heretics in March 1314. They had been in jail and subject to torture for seven years. As soon as they were dead legends began to grow not only around them, but also around the Templar Order. Many of them were unquestionably false rumors, designed to discredit the order.

It was said, for example, that de Molay was actually an immediate descendant of a mysterious Mongol general named Mulay, who had entered Jerusalem in the service of the Ilkhanate ruler Mahmud Ghazan (1271–1304). The Ilkhanate Mongols were Moslems who laid claim to part of the city—and who had discovered a number of strange things in the ruins of the temple, which he later passed down through the various branches of his lineage. (Some of this tale came from a manuscript written by the mysterious Templar of Tyre entitled *Gestes des Chiprios*, and for years this alleged connection confused historians.) One of these "items" was said to be a creature, created by sorcery, which the Templars subsequently held in their fortress at La Covertoirade on the Lanzac Plateau in Southern France. It was here that they allegedly fed on the blood of virgin girls. It was also said that in order to avoid detection this being was transferred to a church in the village of Rennes-le-Chateau in Southern France. It was said that a local priest, Berenger Sauniere, discovered the creature there in the late 1880s and secretly sold it to the Vatican for an extraordinary sum, which enabled him to live a lavish lifestyle. The creature (or some remnant of it) is still said to lie somewhere in the Vatican. The story is almost certainly a falsehood, possibly invented to add to the mystery of Rennes-le-Chateau, and was circulated to discredit de Molay and his order. Apart from such stories, no other evidence regarding this has ever been uncovered and it is certain that Jacques de Molay was not descended from a Mongol general.

The story, however, was given some credibility by the idea that de Molay had supernatural powers and that from the stake he had cursed Philip, the pope, and his entire French Royal line (the Capetian monarchs). It is said that as the flames lit the pyre, de Molay showed no fear and called on God to avenge him on his enemies: the king, the pope, and the Capetian line. Within a year both Clement and Philip were dead—the pope finally succumbing to an illness that had plagued him for years and the monarch from a sudden stroke that killed him while he was out hunting. Following Philip's death the Capetian line began to slowly collapse with two short-lived successors: his grandson, John I, only reigned for five days (November 15, 1316 to November 20, 1316), making his one of the shortest reigns in European history. The decline in the fortunes of the monarchy continued from 1314 to 1328 when the 300-year-old House of Capet finally fell to be succeeded by the House of Valois, which was actually one of its own cadet branches. This gave the common nickname to the rule of the later Capetian monarchs, *Les Rois Maudits* (The Accursed Kings), and their fortunes were linked directly to de Molay's supposed curse. Whether or not he had issued the curse (and there are strong suggestions that he did not), the idea added to the Templar Master's alleged supernatural powers and to some of the tales about him. If he could utter a curse that would bring down an entire royal lineage, ran the argument, could he not also secretly create life in an alembic in some hidden chamber? The idea that the Templars had somehow created monstrous life gradually began take form and grow.

There have been some associations made between the Knight, Templar and the rise of the Freemasons, 400 years after de Molay's death. This was supposed to be somehow linked to the building of Solomon's Temple, over the ruins of which the Templars had charge. The Masons were supposed to have gleaned "wonderful and terrible secrets" from what the Templars had found there and have protected these in their various lodges through the years. Hints and directions leading to such secrets were to be found not in hidden texts, but in the geometry and symmetry of Masonic building and ornamentation, and throughout the years there have been many attempts by non-Masons to decode these and to discover what these supposed "secrets" might be. The linkage between the two orders is probably due to the secrecy that surrounded certain Masonic rituals, coupled with the often perceived clandestine powers that the Masons seemed to enjoy (reminiscent of the Templars in the medieval Church), and from the organization and structure of the Masonic order. As well as this, the inherent mysticism of the Templar order may have appealed to some of the Masons who deliberately sought to connect with them in order to confer mystical status upon themselves. Arguably the most famous connection between the two Orders lies in the construction of the Collegiate Chapel of St. Matthew in Roslin, Midlothian, Scotland, which has recently been made famous in Dan Brown's *The Da Vinci Code*. Rosslyn Chapel, as it is known, was built by William Sinclair, 1st Earl of Caithness (1410–1484), and legend states that it is constructed in the same dimensions and to the same specifications as the Temple of Solomon in Jerusalem, and that it contains a great deal of enigmatic Templar symbolism in its ornamentation. This has led to the assertion that the Sinclair family were Templars and that the structure of the chapel points to a hidden "truth" (as it does in Dan Brown's book), which might be somehow connected with them. In actual fact, the Sinclair family were very active *against* the Templars in Scotland and testified against them in the Scottish Courts in 1309. It is thought that they might even have taken Templar lands as the order was being dissolved. Nevertheless, there was supposedly a connection between Rosslyn Chapel and the Templars, which was linked to Freemasonry; indeed, a philanthropic branch of the Masonic

Lodge in America and some other countries called themselves the Order of the Knights Templar, although in some places it remains at a distance from a main lodge, as it is only open to Christian Masons (in America it remains fairly close, but undertakes what is known as the York Rite).

And there is indeed a connection between the Sinclairs of Roslin and Freemasonry. William Sinclair of Roslin was appointed in 1441 by James II of Scotland as "Chief Patron and Protector" of the Scottish stonemason's guild and to oversee their rites and rituals. The family would remain in that position (which had to be renewed with each Scottish monarch) until James VI—James I of England—neglected to do so, and it partly slid into disuse. It was while they were protectors that certain artifacts were given into the keeping of the Sinclair family—may have included some form of life created by Jacques de Molay. Again, there is no evidence of this, although attempts have been made to find it through the Sinclair papers. In 1736, William Sinclair renounced the patronage of the stonemasons (which had largely been an honorary title for some years), but was immediately elected Grand Master of the lodge of Scottish Freemasons. And of course the legends now persisted that certain Lodges of Freemasons in Scotland secretly held the results of the Templar experiments. Again there is absolutely no evidence for this, and the idea had become what is now referred to as "an urban myth" by those who sought to discredit the Masons, just as others had tried to discredit the Templars. The artificial creature or creatures that the Order of Templars is supposed to have created (if indeed they existed) would appear to have somehow vanished into the mists of time and legend. The Templars were, however, not the only allegedly mystical organization to be accused of clandestinely manufacturing lifeforms.

Mysterious Brotherhoods

Between the years 1607 and 1616, two strange pamphlets appeared in German. Entitled *Fama Fraternitatis R.C.* (The Fame of the Brotherhood of R.C.) and *Confessio Fraternitatis R.C.* (The Confession of the Brotherhood of

R.C.), the works were both mystical and quasi-political both in tone and content. The R.C. in the title stands for Christian Rosenkreuz or Rosenkreutz (Rosy Cross), a shadowy figure who allegedly lived in the 15th century. Throughout the centuries, there has been much speculation as to the identity of this mysterious person both by philosophers and occultists. Some thinkers say that he was born around 1370 into a German family named Germelshausen, which held lands in the Thuringian Forest. The family castle was said to stand deep in the forest on the site of a prehistoric fortress and the family was supposed to be strongly Cathar (the Cathars were a Christian heresy, partly based on Gnosticism). Christian was supposed to be the last descendant of the family—they had been reputedly wiped out because of their beliefs by Konrad von Marburg, Landgrave of Thuringia—and heir to all their secrets and mysteries. This account of course does not stand up to scrutiny. No record of the castle or its family exists, and the name Germelshausen actually comes from an old folktale concerning a cursed village that sank into the ground and only reappears once every seven years. Other thinkers have suggested that the name "Christian Rosenkreuz" might actually be a pseudonym for the English politician and scientist, Francis Bacon (1561–1625), the first (and only) Earl of St. Alban who dabbled in all sorts of scientific enquiry.

Rosenkreuz had died allegedly aged 106 years old, but before that he had traveled to many parts of the world and had learned many strange and secret things. He was said to have sat at the feet of Arab, Persian, and Turkish teachers, as well as Sufi and Zoroastrian masters, and had studied "ancient mysteries from Egypt." On returning to Europe, he had founded a society of eight mages called "The Fraternity of the Rose Cross" (FRC), together with a holy house known as the *Sanctus Spiritus* (The House of the Holy Spirit), which was supposedly designed from the Temple of Solomon in Jerusalem. No location is given for this place, but it was here that Rosenkreuz went to die and where his body was supposedly found by certain followers more than 120 years after his death (which occurred in the utmost secrecy) in an uncorrupted state. Still other sources say that

Christian Rosenkreuz never died at all, but turned up hundreds of years later as the Comte de St. Germaine.

The pamphlets that appeared in Germany called for "the Universal Reformation of Mankind" and suggested that there was a secret society of mystics (technically "mystic-doctors"), who would be able to bring this about. It was said that Rosenkreuz had recruited seven friends who were as skilled and knowledgeable of mystic ways as he was, who were sworn to secrecy (each was a sworn bachelor to prevent spouses or families from finding out) and who would aid the sick and cure ills mainly by mystical or alchemical means. Each one also swore to find a replacement for himself before his death to perpetuate the society. Indeed there had been rumors—little more than tales—of just such a body circulating in Germany for many years before, but there had been no proof—now these texts seemed to give credence to at least some of the stories.

Although the pamphlets (or "manifestos" as they were called) were treated as a hoax by the authorities, they caused something of a furor as they spread throughout Europe. This interest was further stimulated in 1622 when a series of posters began to appear on the streets of Paris proclaiming the existence of a secret brotherhood who were watching the society and who were probably protecting ancient secrets, which could either help or destroy the world. In many respects this "secret society of mages" resembled the Secret Masters of H.P. Blavatsky, that number of sages who dwelt in far-away Tibet but who were aware, through mystical means, of the world beyond. The society founded by Christian Rosenkreuz, (supposedly around 1604), however, practiced both medicine and alchemy and its members were adepts in both. Throughout the mid-1600s, interest in this mysterious society slowly began to grow, attracting many of the thinkers, early scientists, and physicians of the time.

One of those who became intrigued by the idea was the German physician and alchemist Heinrich Khunrath (1560–1605). Born in Leipzig and deeply interested in the occult, Khunrath was familiar with the tales of a clandestine order of mystics who had experimented with healing processes, the transmutation of metals, and the creation of artificial life. His major work, *Amphiteathrum Sapentiae Aeternae* (The Alchemist's Laboratory—published in Hamburg in 1609 after his death, although a date of 1595 is also given), was heavily influenced by such an idea. This, in turn, influenced another notable figure of the time—the English mathematician, astrologer, astronomer, and occultist, Dr. John Dee (1527–1608/9), who was also a consultant to Queen Elizabeth I.

Even today, Dee remains something of an enigmatic figure. His interests drew together the worlds of magic and science which, during his lifetime, were gradually separating into two disciplines. The son of a gentleman servant at the court of Henry VII, he entered St. John's College in Cambridge in 1542, aged 15 years old, graduating with a BA in 1544. So great was his intellectual ability in the field of mathematics that in 1546 he was made a Founding Fellow of Trinity College and became noticed as a leading English intellectual. The year 1547 found him teaching in both Holland and France, where it is said that he became interested in the occult and hermetic philosophy and began to study some of the works of Hermes Trismegistus. He took a keen interest in magic and during the reign of Mary I (Mary Tudor, 1553–1558) he was arrested in 1553 and imprisoned at Hampton Court for "concocting a sorcerous potion" in an alleged attempt to poison the queen. This had probably more to do with Dee attempting to cast a horoscope for Mary's half-sister Elizabeth (later Elizabeth I) in order to find out the date of the queen's death. In 1555, Dee was released, but was almost immediately rearrested for heresy. He was released again in 1556, this time with Mary's full pardon.

When Mary's half-sister Elizabeth I came to the throne in 1558, Dee's fortunes improved considerably. Indeed, he became something of a court consultant on arcane matters and was even asked to predict the most auspicious time for the new queen's coronation. It was even rumored that he was a secret agent for the new regime and that he was centrally involved in Elizabethan politics. However, there were still whisperings against him concerning witchcraft and alchemy, and there seems little doubt that his interest in the occult increased. He began to travel on the Continent once again (some believe that this was on spying business for the English court) and once again seemed to immerse himself in mystical thinking. In 1564, he published a major work on the occult, *Monas Heiroglyphica*, which contained a number of symbols and drawings that Dee asserted were the "true sum of hidden knowledge." Following this, he produced several other books that he also said represented "secret intelligences from the world of spirits," which have been subsequently pored over by students of the occult. On returning to England he was asked to evaluate the portent of certain comets that had been seen in the skies over England.

It was frequently assumed that John Dee was one of the adepts who had been recruited into the organization of mystics by Christian Rosenkreuz, and which was now allegedly taking the name Rosicrucians (the Brotherhood of the Rosy-Cross) in his honor. It was thought that under their influence Dee was introduced to alchemy and the formation of life. Although he is more associated (along with his later assistant Edward Kelly) with attempts to contact disembodied spirits, once more the old ideas of artificially created creatures living in jars began to circulate around him. It is said that if Dee was a spy, he used some of these beings to do part of his work for him, hiding away in shadowy corners and reporting on conversations they heard.

John Dee was not the only thinker to be influenced by the idea of a secret society like the Rosicrucians. In Germany, the thinker Michael Maier (1568–1622) also became intrigued by the existence of the secret Rosicrucian Order. Maier was an extremely learned and influential man and was Court Physician to the Hapsburg prince Rudolf II. He was also an alchemist who had not only been trying to transmute metals into gold, but also (it was rumored) trying to create life. Although allegedly not one himself, he wrote several defenses of the adepts, and, in 1617, he produced an emblem book—the *Atalanta Furgiens*—which he presented to his patron Rudolf. This book was said to include alchemic symbols for a number of wondrous things. An emblem book was a collection of pictorial images, each symbolizing a deeper truth, with an explanation for each. Maier suggested that the images within the book represented certain hidden wisdoms of Hermes Trismegistus and that they held alchemical truths. It was said that he had created "life of a sort" using the formulae that the images symbolized, and that others might follow his example if they could follow the mystical truths contained therein. Such theories seem to have proved too radical for Rudolf, but it is possible that others may have sought to develop the alchemical directions.

Around the same time, there were others, apart from Maier, who were also fascinated by the concept of Rosicrucianism. The English mathematician and astronomer Robert Fludd (1574–1637), for instance, though not claiming to be a member of the order himself, wrote a long and detailed defense of it entitled *Apologia Compendiana* in 1616. Although Fludd was allegedly one of the "Divines" who worked on the King James version of the Bible, similar to John Dee he was strongly associated with dark magic and witchcraft. Indeed, so strong were the suspicions against him that he was prevented from being admitted as a Fellow of St. John's College Oxford (he was not admitted until 1609)—although it may be that the college found him arrogant and offensive. Fludd proclaimed himself to be a follower of Paracelsus, which was the name adopted by Theophratus Phillippus Aureolus Bombastus von Hohenheim (1493–1541). The name he assumed meant "greater than Celsus" and refers to the Roman encyclopaedist Aulus Cornelius Celsus, who allegedly wrote the first medical treatise. He formed a small society that claimed to have the key to Universal Science, derived from Paracelsus's work. Part of this Key lay in alchemic pursuits and, like many before him, Fludd claimed to have created some sort of life in a copper beaker. However, as his interest in Rosicrucianism grew, he abandoned his own society and began to write in defense of the Rosicrucians. His work circulated widely throughout Europe inspiring a number of others. One of these was Thomas Vaughan (1621–1666), a Welsh thinker who founded yet another small group dedicated to occult and mystic matters: the Society of Unknown Philosophers. This group was centered on the works of Paracelsus and through it Vaughan translated some of the works of the Rosicrucians into English. In 1652, he translated the *Fama Fraternitatis* together with some other texts that were supposed to be the unknown writings of Hermes Trismegistus. These reputedly dealt with such topics as the Philosopher's Stone and the creation of life. Slightly later, Vaughan began to work with Dr. Robert Child, with whom he set up a "chemical club," which consisted of an archive and a working laboratory with the aim of collecting ancient texts concerning the transmutation of metals and the creation of artificial life. According to legend, Child created some form of life, which is hinted at in several texts written under the name Eugenius Philalethes (clearly a pseudonym) that began to appear in the late 1650s. Some have argued that it was Child who penned these, and that it was actually Vaughan; to add to the confusion, some of these may have been forgeries written slightly later by Robert Samber (1682–1745), a notorious Freemason who is famous for writing the celebrated pamphlet *In Praise of Drunkenness.* Although it is known that neither Vaughan nor Child ever found the Philosopher's Stone and their supposed creation of artificial life is questionable, their writings (and those of other thinkers and academics) did keep both alchemical practice and the possibility of finding and creating such things very much to the fore.

In 1616 a curious and anonymous document suddenly appeared, again in Germany (this time in Stuttgart), which was perhaps related to Rosicrucianism and to alchemy. It was entitled *The Chymical Wedding of Christian Rosenkreutz,* and although its author was unknown, it was suspected to be a German churchman named Johannes Valentinus Andreae (1586–1654). This cleric had graduated with a degree in theology from the University at Tubingen and became a deacon in Vaihaingen an der Enz before becoming a priest in the town of Calw in 1620. He was considered something of a radical and often had an "offensive manner" about him. Andreae eventually became a preacher at the court in Stuttgart where he spoke of radical reform of the Church. It is also thought that is where he published the *Chymical Wedding* that had been greatly influenced by (and gave great credence to) the secret Brotherhood of the Rosicrucians. Although the pamphlet appeared in Stuttgart, it was apparently edited in Strasburg, and the significance of this location is not lost, because it was here that early editions of the German Bible (the Gutenburg Bible) also appeared. And the account is littered with passages from the Bible—particularly the New Testament—which points toward an amalgamation of both Jewish and Christian mystical thinking. It also, incidentally, makes a connection with Dr. John Dee's *Monas Heiroglyphica* and other Hermetic manuscripts.

The text is an allegorical tale that is reputedly packed with secret symbolism. It is divided into seven days and seven nights, similar to the biblical book of Genesis, and is said to rely heavily on the early Hebrew teaching—some say Kabbalistic teachings, although these have been fused with esoteric Christian symbols (for example, the Nine Lords who also attend the wedding correspond with books of the Bible). It is reputedly set in the year 1459 (the end of the seventh day), which links it to the Freemasons of Strasburg who signed their constitution at Ravensburg on Easter of that year. In the story Christian Rosenkreuz is invited to go to a wonderful castle, to attend the sacred wedding of a king and a queen. While there he is invited to help in the actual wedding and goes through a number of procedures in order to do this. Many scholars read a secret meaning into this, claiming that it represented a series of initiation ceremonies into the Rosicrucians or into some secret society of alchemists. The wedding concludes satisfactorily and all of the guests are given a piece of gold "as a remembrance." The symbolism of alchemical triumph is obvious.

The *Chymical Wedding* was supposed to be one of the great manifestos of the secret Brotherhood of Rosicrucians, and if it was indeed Andreae (whose name was linked to it when he was the abbot of the evangelical monastic school in Adelberg) then the Church took a dim view of the matter. At first he denied it, but would later admit to it in his later memoirs just before his death. However, he did not discuss the full importance of the work or what some of the curious symbolism contained in it actually meant. Later students of the work have interpreted it as containing secret instructions for the creation of gold, others for the creation of life. This text, together with a number of others that had appeared, only advanced the idea in the public mind that groups of alchemists were working secretly on all sorts of strange experiments, which might even include the formation of life or indeed of new forms of life.

Indeed, as the 17th century progressed and science gradually began to separate itself from the magic of former years, it seemed that alchemists were everywhere, either working alone or in clandestine societies. This feeling was not to dissipate for a long time (we still have echoes of it today in many modern conspiracy theories). Much was made of these individuals and groupings either using or being the guardians of "hidden knowledge" or "the wisdom of the ancients" (a belief which still has resonance today). Thinkers and intellectuals began to study the works of earlier alchemists such as Nicolas Flamel, scanning them for hidden meaning. Flamel (1330–1418) was an unremarkable French bookseller who supposedly acquired an ancient text written on tree bark in an unknown language and supposedly penned by someone styled as "Abraham the Jew." He had already studied some alchemy and was convinced that what he held in his hands was an important and mysterious work from some ancient time. Believing part of the text to be in Hebrew, Flamel traveled to Spain where he met up with an old scholar, Maestro Canches, who returned to France with him and worked on the book. He later became very wealthy, and it is said that he found the Philosopher's Stone and also the secret of creating life. Because of this Flamel is regarded as one of the greatest alchemists of all time and is reputed to have left a series of mystical texts. At the center of such study were the Rosicrucians and the Freemasons (Scottish Freemasonry in particular was thought to have been closely associated with the Rosicrucian movement). The Rosicrucian movement was now supposed to have grown well beyond the original eight members that Christian Rosenkreuz had gathered around him.

Secret Experiments

Around the end of the 19th and the beginning of the 20th centuries, interest in secret societies and ancient wisdom seemed to resurface. Once again Rosicrucianism came to the fore, although this time in three seemingly separate strands. The first of these was as a kind of Christian mysticism that treated Christianity as a mystery religion in the style of the early Church fathers; another was a Masonic strand that traced its roots back to the Regius Manuscript, supposedly written around 1390, which is said to be one of the oldest texts in Freemasonry. The third strand was the Ancient and Mystical Order of Rosicrucians (AMORC), formed in 1915 and supposed to devote itself to the uncovering of ancient philosophical and mystical truths, which included alchemy and the creation of life. Its roots were (and still are) said to lie in ancient Egyptian texts. It was even rumoured that some of the modern-day Rosicrucians were engaged in the sciences and that some worked for American government projects with regard to cloning and stem-cell research. There were even rumours of societies *within* societies—the most famous being the Priory of Sion, which was linked with Rosicrucianism and is featured in Dan Brown's book *The Da Vinci Code.* This too was supposedly a grouping guarding ancient secrets that were best kept from the world, and Brown's modern fiction has only added to that myth. The idea of a secret society of alchemists working to create some hideous lifeform that might one day swamp the world really hasn't gone away.

Many of the ancient scientists divided all elements in the world into two kinds—male and female. It was suggested that if certain elements came together in a way that simulated human sexual congress then, just as in human reproduction, life might be created. Fluids or forces added to inert elements might act in the same way as human semen, creating the starting spark of strange and terrible life. Many of the ancient allegorical texts that the ancient writers put out are suggestive of this point. By bringing these elements together life might be created, even though it might not be human life. The idea of some "thing" lurking in its shadowy jar—the monstrous homunculus—seems to have been in many of their thoughts.

Mandrakes

There was one plant that fascinated the medieval alchemists and may have had something to do with the idea of the homunculus. A member of the nightshade family, the mandrake seemed to have many qualities that resembled those of humankind. The branched, parsnip-shaped root, for example, was said to sometimes look like a human body, which gave it its nickname "little man," and it was supposed to make a sound whenever it was pulled from the earth that resembled the cry of a human being in pain. It had hallucinogenic properties and may have been used extensively in dark magic and witchcraft. Mandrakes had fascinated humans since biblical times. Among the early Semites, they were considered a cure for infertility in women, as is witnessed by the story of Ruben and Leah in the book of Genesis (Genesis 30:14–22). References to their "love-making" properties and their powers at making barren women fertile are to be found in numerous Hebrew texts, including the Song of Solomon. All aspects of the plant were, however, poisonous, so the stories of "love philtres" that had been made from either its root or its fruit are completely erroneous.

Later general folklore (which was often accepted by the alchemists) suggested that the mandrake was a combination of two elements, both human and plant. It was said that human semen spilled upon the ground (particularly if that semen was that of a hanged criminal, ejaculated at the moment of death), would cause a mandrake to grow on the spot where it fell. Consequently the mandrake was part human, and when its root was dug up, it would scream like a human being and those who heard it would instantly die. Indeed, certain complicated protections were performed in order to avoid hearing the mandrake's "death cry" when unearthing it. For instance, the Hebrew writer Josephus (AD 37–c. 100), advises that a furrow must first be dug around the man-shaped root of the plant and that a dog should be tied to the root itself. The person must then run away, and when the dog attempts to follow and inadvertently pulls up the root the dog hears the scream and dies instead of the person. The sagely Julian of Norwich (c. 1342–c. 1416) advised stopping one's ears with a waxy preparation before pulling the root in order to remain oblivious to the deadly sound. The root might then be safely used in the preparation of magic potions and philtres.

Alchemical connections between the mandrake root and the homunculus were so strong that in many instances the image of the alchemist about to create life often also includes that of the mandrake in a bottle as part of the scientist's impedimenta. Paracelsus also refers to the root as "the little man in the bottle." The root was also referred to as the Mandragora, which, it was said, might be the basis of artificial life, but the Mandragora also had sorcerous powers in its own right. To make a Mandragora it was not always necessary to have a mandrake root. According to several ancient herbals and grimoires one should take a spring of bryony and bury it in the grave of a newly deceased man. It should then be fed on blood and milk and at the end of 30 days (or sometimes between full moons) it should be dug up again when it might have the semblance of life about it or manifest supernatural protective powers if carried about one's person.

The homunculus in the jar was, however, not the only creature that the alchemists were said to have created by artificial means. There were rumors that some of these early scientists had also created "simulacra" in their laboratories. The term *simulacrum* comes from a Latin word meaning "likeness" and in early times was meant to suggest an exact double. In the later modern period (the 18th and 19th centuries) it was a philosophical concept, but in the late 19th century it came to mean "an image which, while having the likeness of the original, lacked the substance." It was, therefore, an inferior being created artificially. Many stories—all of them probably without any basis—exist concerning attempts (both successful and unsuccessful) of alchemists who had tried to make the image of living men.

Ramon Llull

One such tale concerns the great medieval Majorcan thinker and teacher Ramon Llull (1232–1315), who was at one time tutor to the future James II of Aragon. Although he is probably better known as a mathematician and as a philosopher, there are stories that Llull dabbled in the occult as well as alchemy. It is also said that he was greatly interested in creating a semblance of life—the imperfect man—but due to his position at court, he kept such work a secret. Nevertheless, he wrote several treatises on alchemy and mathematics (his most famous work being the *Ars Magna,* which was published in 1305), some of which have survived until today.

It was said that whenever Llull traveled (and in his early years he seems to have led something of an itinerant lifestyle), he was often accompanied by a manservant who never spoke. The servant accompanied him, even after he had a religious experience and became a tertiary Franciscan; it was noted that he never seemed to age. Nevertheless, he often appeared rather brutish and uncouth and many people were more than a little frightened of him. At the court of one of the Spanish Catalan kings, the ruler is said to have asked Llull about the servant (previously the scientist had never spoken about him or of his origins). Llull told the monarch, confidentially, that although giving the appearance of humanity, the being was in fact not human at all, but a kind of simulacrum that he had "grown" in his laboratory from something he called a *luffah* or *beid-el-jinn* (djinn's egg—thought to be a mandrake root or something similar), which he had obtained in the Middle East during some earlier travels. (Incidentally the luffah to which Llull referred may be the fruit of a subtropical vine that can be eaten, but when dried, acquires a spongy consistency; it is the origin of our word *loo-fah*, used in the bath). It had no power to speak of, having "neither a voice or the means of making one." He also confided to the monarch that the creature never slept, and that it had a limited intelligence (thus showing that it was less that perfect), and that it only responded to direct orders. It was therefore fit for little else but servitude. At any time, Llull told the astonished king, he could return this being to the dust out of which it had been created. Moreover, he had originally based the features of the being on a man whom he had known back in Majorca, and it had looked relatively civilized, but as time had gone on, the image had grown coarser and more bestial, perhaps denoting the lack of a soul. After Llull's death around 1315, the servant seems to have disappeared and no one knows what became of him—perhaps the alchemist had already destroyed him.

Edward Kelley

The story of Ramon Llull's unspeaking servant is paralleled in several other tales concerning alchemists, including the English John Dee and Roger Bacon (an early scientist concerned with the creation of life both alchemical and mechanical). Legend says that Dee's associate, the allegedly disreputable Edward Kelley, created such simulacra as assistants somewhere around the late 1500s. These almost mindless creatures had allegedly aided Kelley with some of his own alchemical work in the search for transmutation of metals. Kelley may have boasted of creating such simulacra, but it must be remembered that he was very prone to exaggeration, especially about his alchemical and magical prowess. Similar stories were told of Roger Bacon, but as with Kelley, none of them were ever proven. Similar to the homunculus, the simulacra remains a mystery of the medieval alchemical period, as science and magic started to go their separate ways.

Eastern Creations

Although much of the experimentation regarding the creation of artificial life appears to have taken place among the alchemists in Western Europe, a somewhat similar process, albeit with slightly different outcomes, was taking place among the mystics of the East. In the high lamaseries of places such as Tibet it is said that monks were able to create thought forms that took on some form of material manifestation. These beings were known as *tulpa*, derived from the Sanskrit word meaning "to build or construct," and often took on a form that we might equate with ghosts or poltergeists. They were created, not by alchemical or material means, but by sustained mental energies, and only the greatest lamas or yogic masters could produce them. In essence they seem to be corporeal thought-forms that were, initially at least, created and motivated by the energies of those who brought them into being. In many cases the tulpa (when it did take concrete form) actually often resembled its creator, and there was a specific reason for this. In the past, many of the great lamas sought to cheat death, and so they created a likeness of themselves in order to fool the Grim Reaper, which would then take the simulacrum and leave the master unmolested. However, the energies used to create and maintain a tulpa were immense and the creator had to be extremely careful, for as the being gained more and more substance, so its consciousness and will began to grow. Soon it might even become independent from its creator. This idea forms the basis of an old Tibetan folktale.

∽

A selfish man who lived near the monastery at La-Chen did not wish to die, and had heard that if one made a tulpa he might be able to fool Yama [a god of death], who would take the creature

instead of him and he would be spared. However, he did not have the power to create such a thing himself, so he went to the monastery where there was a very holy man living to see if he could fool him as well. He told the sage that he wished to create a double in order to do good works on his behalf, so that he could double his efforts to help the poor as the ancient Buddhist texts taught. The holy man was not fooled, but agreed to help him, and with great energy created a tulpa, which was very close to the image of the greedy man.

"Now," said the sage, "all that you are will go into this being, and if you are true as you say it will be a blessing to you, but if you are not, then it will be the worse for you, for although I have fashioned it for you, this is *your* creation. This is my warning to you." But the greedy man took no account of the sagely words and kept the tulpa close by him. No matter where this man went, the double followed him at a distance in case Yama would come upon him unexpectedly. He used it only for evil and for accessing wealth, despite what he had told the holy man. Through time the being began to grow in both strength and substance. It grew like a plant or like a shadow in strong sun. And as it grew, it received a will and intelligence of its own. One day when the man told it to do something—to take some rice from a neighbor—it refused and turned upon him. It seized him by the throat and threatened to choke him.

"Why are you doing this?" the man spluttered. "Am I not your master and did I not call you into life?"

"You are no master to me!" the tulpa replied. "For I indeed *am* you. Had you done good things and had you been less wicked and greedy, I would have reflected this, but now I am only filled with envy and greed. *You* are to blame for my state." And so it choked the man and delivered him to Yama, because he had no power over it and had no way to stop it. And the tulpa lived out its days as the man—for none knew the difference—and all that he had acquired through his lust and greed it took as its own. This was a punishment that the holy man in the monastery at La-Chen had foreseen."

In the moral tale, the tulpa appears to be almost like a sponge and it grows and develops, taking on many of the characteristics of the individual who has created it or who commands it. This, in some traditions, is indeed one of the attributes of the being—it can sometimes be used for good (when it takes on beneficial characteristics) or more frequently for evil (when the opposite occurs). In most cases, however, the tulpa does not achieve full material status, but remains as a disembodied energy/thought-form.

Just to complicate matters a little further, in some parts of Tibet the term *tul-pa* or *sprul-pa* can refer to the *essence* of a magician or sorcerer-monk (the essence of a Grand Lama such as the Dalai, Panchen, or Tashi Lamas is specifically referred to as a *tulku*—a reincarnation lineage—which can sometimes merge (perhaps as a thought-form) with another person or object. For example, the wife of Marpa, the great guru (teacher) and follower of Milarepa, the Tibetan Buddhist saint, finished her days as a thought-form or tulpa that finally amalgamated with the corporeal body of her husband. This is in the tradition of "mind transmission" as allegedly practiced by some gurus and sages in the high Himalayas. Similar beliefs occur on the Siberian Steppe where certain local shamans among the Karagas and Taigi peoples are also said to have the power to amalgamate their spirits (usually at the point of death) with others whom they know, thus creating an altogether new person. This is also done (as in the Himalayas) in the form of a "mindstream" or flow of consciousness.

The idea of creating or "growing" a person, either by alchemical means or through thought and imagination, appears in a number of disparate cultures and perhaps addresses a common question in the human consciousness: Can Man create life in the way that either evolution or a Supreme

Creator has done? It is the answer to this question that perhaps the medieval alchemists and Eastern mystics strove to find. Perhaps it is a question that we in our scientific world are still trying to resolve, even today. Maybe we have not altogether forgotten the mysterious thing in the jar.

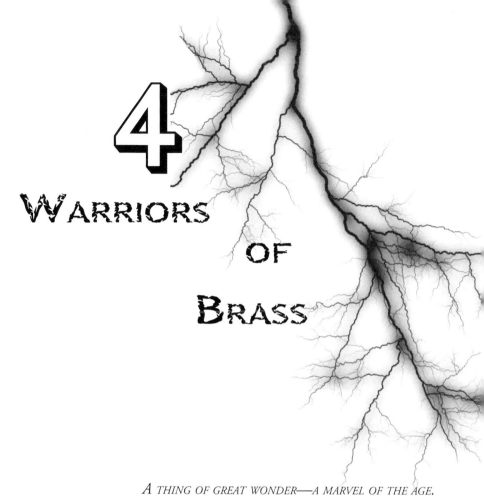

4
WARRIORS
OF
BRASS

A THING OF GREAT WONDER—A MARVEL OF THE AGE.

—ANONYMOUS ENGLISH WRITER DESCRIBING THE 1377 CROWNING OF
KING RICHARD II BY A SPECIALLY BUILT MECHANICAL ANGEL

THERE IS AN INTERESTING if unlikely tale concerning the medieval inventor, philosopher, and Franciscan friar Roger Bacon (1214–1294). Bacon, who was widely known as "Dr. Mirabilis" (Latin for "astounding doctor") had been a professor at Oxford University and had also traveled extensively on the Continent. There he had learned "the ways of the Arabs," and had studied their mathematics and sciences, including that of mechanics. Using theories derived from the latter, he constructed a man's head made of brass, which he said could speak and prognosticate many future events. However, it would only speak when it was ready, and then only when it was directly answered. For a long time, the brass head remained silent; so he would not miss its utterance Bacon left a young novice to watch while he rested. In some other versions of the story he leaves a colleague, Friar Bungay, to watch. The addition of Bungay may be the result of a comedic stage play *The Honourable History of Friar Bungay and Friar Bacon* written around 1588 by Robert Greene, which linked the two characters together). Bacon told the boy that the head would be able to speak three times and would signal when it was ready by saying something. When he first spoke the boy was to rouse Bacon, who would then come and question it. The boy sat down and waited, but the head remained silent. Gradually, the heat from a nearby fire made the boy drowsy and he dozed off. The head stirred to life—its eyes flashed and it spoke. "Time was," it observed in a metallic voice. By this time the boy was sound asleep and the head fell silent again. After a while, the eyes flashed once more and the head spoke again. "Time is," it said. The boy slumbered on. At length, the eyes flashed one final time. "Time will be," said the head, and as there was no one to question it, it fell silent forever. Friar Bacon awoke and came in to inspect the situation. Finding the boy asleep and realising what must have happened, he was furious. He berated the youth, telling him that he'd probably lost one of the greatest scientific opportunities of the age and in all the world. And, although he tried many times to do so, Friar Bacon never got the brass head to speak again, and in the end simply kept it as an ornament. This tale probably did not happen, but it does serve to illustrate the ancient world's fascination with mechanisms and with the possibility of early robots.

Although both science fiction and science fact have encouraged us to think of robots as being of fairly modern origin, there is much evidence to suggest that they were being thought of in early civilizations. References to metal men and women appear in stories and legends from both ancient Greece and Rome.

Greek Legends

In Greek legend, for example, the lame blacksmith god Hephaestus (Vulcan in Roman mythology) made two beings out of gold. Hephaestus was the son of Zeus by the goddess Hera, who at the time of his birth was in a quarrel with the god. The child was born extremely ugly, and in a fit of rage Hera hurled it from Olympus and into the ocean, damaging its leg on some rocks. The infant was washed up on the shores of the island of Lemnos where it was cared for by the Sintians, an ancient Lemnian tribe who nursed him back to full health. However, he was now lame and found it difficult to get about the island. It is said that from the Cyclops who were living on Lemnos at the time, he learned the art of blacksmithing (the Cyclops were considered to be skilled metalworkers) and was able to construct two tiny golden servants for himself who assisted him around the island. These supposed characters, both of them female, were considered a wonder by many ancient writers. Describing them in his work *The Illiad* (Book 18), the Greek poet Homer states: "They were golden handmaids also who worked for him and were like real young women with sense and reason, voice also and strength and all the learning of the immortals."

The connection between Hephaestus and mechanized figures did not end with his tiny servants, however. Instructed by Zeus to defend the island of Crete, Hephaestus forged a "copper giant" named Thalos. This corresponded to a gigantic humanoid shape with two "horns" emerging from its head like antennae in order to enable it to "see." A single artery filled with a "black blood" ran from the crown of the copper man's head to the heel of one of its feet, which was plugged by a stopper. It patrolled the coastline of Crete for a number of years, protecting it from any form of invasion. When such invasion took place, Thalos could emit streams of fire in order to scatter and defeat them. It could also hurl rocks at enemy ships if they ventured too close to the shore, and it became a mouthpiece for Minos, the tyrant-king of Crete. Some of Crete's enemies, however, employed the sorceress Medea, who misled Thalos with "false visions". As the copper giant blundered about

chasing spurious phantoms, several enemy soldiers managed to extract the stopper from its heel, allowing a thick, black viscous "blood" to drain into the ground. Gradually, Thalos began to weaken and was soon overcome by the invading forces. The great copper body was broken up and the head carried away as a trophy by the victors (possibly back to Athens with which Crete was at war). From then on, the country became particularly vulnerable to invasion.

In many ways the idea of Thalos corresponds with the image of the menacing robot, which has appeared in a number of modern sci-fi books and movies—big, automated, and with two great horns that resembled antennae on either side of its head. It was allegedly the supreme defense mechanism created by the lame son of a god to maintain a bloody and barbaric tyrant on his throne.

The stories about Hephaestus were, of course, imaginary—they are the stuff of Greek mythology (although the legend of Thalos might well be based on *something* in the ancient world)—but they may have reflected some of the work that was going on throughout the ancient world regarding the creation of life-like mechanisms. The idea of Pygmalion, the Cypriot sculptor who carved a beautiful woman out of ivory, fell in love with it, and magically brought it to life, may well have hinted at the ancients preoccupation with bringing mechanical beings to "life." One of the earliest actual accounts we have of a working automaton is that of a mechanical pigeon that could move its wings and was created by the astronomer and engineer Archytas of Tarentum (420–356 BC). Archytas, who had studied the works of either the Greek mathematician Pythagoras or Phiolaus (a Phythagoran mathematician 470–385 BC), created a number of such toys—some depending on a sequence of gears and pulleys. (Indeed it was Archytas who developed the pulley in ancient engineering.) Powered by steam, the pigeon (made of wood and metal) was said to have flown 200 feet before falling to the earth—although the veracity of this is uncertain. Archytas was also said to have invented a rattle that could vibrate and amuse infants. One of his friends and disciples was the celebrated philosopher Plato.

Although Archytas made one of the first *recorded* robotic mechanisms, it is quite possible that there were others in the early world who made such devices. Indeed, Archytas may have copied some of the inventors in the Middle East or even further away in China. Here it is thought that some early engineers had experimented with kites to produce mechanised flying things (Archytas is also known to have experimented with kites). And there were also stories (perhaps some of them imaginary) of Chinese inventors and engineers creating beings that closely resembled the Greek Thalos.

Chinese Legends

In some Chinese legends reference is made to the Chi-Yu, a fantastic "dragon" that lived in the "inhospitable mountains" (although exactly when it lived there is unknown). This was quite clearly an automated device as it had a metallic coat with four eyes and six arms with which it negotiated the broken terrain of its area. According to the ancient tales it was fed on rock, which provided the energy for it to move forward. Just who built this amazing construction is unknown, but it was said to have been made by "great sages" (whoever they were). When the creature "died," its head was taken and placed in a cave in the mountains where it became an object of worship and pilgrimage. From time to time, as pilgrims drew close, some of its eyes would flash and it would emit great clouds of steam, as if to suggest that part of it was still conscious and creating the idea that it had been some sort of "dragon." It was a source of wonder for many years until the cavern where it lay was apparently sealed up. It may well be still there, lost to the world and deep in a cave somewhere in the Chinese mountains.

Technology

One theory concerning the "dragon" was that it was some form of device used for quarrying, and that it may have been guided by a form of a relatively primitive computer. Although we tend to think of computers as modern devices, there is certainly evidence that they were in use long before the birth of Christ. A number of references and remains of computer-like devices have been found dating back to beyond the first century BC, the most famous being the Antikytherea Mechanism, which was discovered at the beginning of the 20th century.

Returning from a sponge-diving expedition on the African coast late in 1900, Greek Captain Dimitrios Kondos and his crew were delayed by a series of storms that were traveling along the Greek coastline. The captain decided to weigh anchor just beyond the storm zone near the island of Antikytherea, where they could do some more diving.

One of the first divers down was Elias Stadatios, who returned with a story concerning a large wreck of an ancient ship that was lying on the sea-bottom, 60 meters down, not far from their anchorage. There were the bodies of men and horses down there, he told Kondos, who at first did not believe him. However, he too went down and came up with some artifacts from the wreck including a bronze arm. Kondos reported the find and divers from the Hellenic Navy together with academics from the Greek Ministry for Education were soon excavating the wreck and bringing up statues and other artifacts. One of the divers, an archaeologist named Vario Stais, noticed some machinery lodged in a nearby rock. He investigated further and found what appeared to be the remains of an ancient device, which he at first believed to be a form of timepiece—the first clock to be discovered. However, further study has shown it to be a rudimentary analogue computer, and its complexity suggests that it may have been one of a number of such devices, the others of which have since been lost. Its construction seems to suggest that it was used for the purposes of astronomy and of celestial measurement, and that it may have been built on the island of Rhodes where the Greek Stoic philosopher and mathematician Posidonius had an academy. (The Stoics were the followers of Zeno of Citium in Cypress, who had originally taught a form of logic at the Stoa Pikile—the Painted Door—from which they got their name. Their logic, which influenced early mathematics, was different from the logic taught by Aristotle.) The mechanism is thought to have been the work of the mathematician and astronomer Hipparchus (190–120 BC), one of the leading Greek scientists of the age. Pieces of the mechanism may still be scattered about the ocean floor, because a series of violent deaths from the "bends" among the divers put an end to any further exploration.

But what was the ancient computer used for, and why was it on a ship heading out of Antikytherea (possibly bound for Rome)? It is thought that the mechanism was used for determining and measuring the positions of stars and planets and coordinating them with the various years around the Mediterranean. This was a device for calculating time and space. The ship that it was on may have belonged to the fleet of the Roman general Lucius Cornelius Sulla. It is also thought that this may have been booty taken by Sulla during his expeditions during the Mithridatic Wars (a conflict between Rome and Mithridates VI of Pontus during the first century BC). The general may have captured it as a prize and was taking it back to Rome when disaster overtook his ship. The Roman writer Lucian recounts how part of Sulla's fleet foundered and sank off the coast of Antikytherea on its way back to Rome, and the wreckage certainly looks as if it might have been part of that fleet.

The Antikytherea Mechanism, ancient though it is, may not be the oldest computer that we know about. Cicero in his *De Republica* speaks of at least two other similar computers that had been captured by another Roman general—Marcus Claudius Marcellus—during a siege at Syracuse in 212 BC, more than a hundred years before the mechanism sank. Both these mechanisms were designed by the great Greek mathematician Archimedes. The siege was part of an ongoing conflict that lasted from 214 to 212 BC between Rome and the area of Magna Graecia, which was located in southern Italy around the Tarentine Gulf and the coast of Sicily, which had been settled by Greek immigrants. The city of Syracuse was an important one and its inhabitants had hired Archimedes to construct a number of defenses that may have been linked to the early computers in some way. Marcellus had great respect for Archimedes and ordered him to be spared at the end of the siege (an order that was ignored—the mathematician was killed as soon as the siege ended). The Roman general took both devices, which were supposedly used for calculating movements of the heavens (important in astrological forecasts) and also for defensive troop movements back to the Imperial City. One of them he kept as an heirloom and the other he gave as an offering at the Temple of Virtus. What became of both these ancient devices is unknown. It is possible, as some have suggested, that they were nothing more than fabrications (and idle boasts) dreamed up by Archimedes, and yet others are not so sure. Pappus of Alexandria (AD 290–350, one of the greatest Greek mathematicians of the ancient world) states that Archimedes wrote a long text (now lost) entitled *On Sphere-Making*, which detailed the construction of the machine and its uses, but to date no other reference to this has been found. (It might have been destroyed with other documents during the burning of the great Library at Alexandria by Julius Caesar in AD 48). But other references to the actual mechanisms remain. Devices such as the Antikytherea Mechanism are mentioned in the works of the Roman writers Lactantus and Proclus, and suggest that the instances of early computers may be more widespread than we imagined—at least four computers (including those designed by Archimedes) are mentioned.

In the early Islamic world, too, computers seem to have made an appearance. The 11th-century *Kitab Al-Hyal* (The Book of Ingenious Devices) attributed to the Banu Musa brothers, records the construction of such an apparatus somewhere around the year AD 1000. The Banu Musa were three 9th-century Muslim brothers—Abu Ja'far Muhammad ibn Shakir (803–873) Ahmad Mosa ibn Shakir (803–873), and Hasan ibn Shakir

(810–873), who are still considered to be the greatest mathematicians and inventors of early Islam. All of their works are virtually indistinguishable from one another, so it is difficult to say which of them invented what particular mechanism or exactly when they died (the dates of their deaths are linked together, perhaps for convenience), and so a common date has been accorded to them. Their text gives many wonderful inventions (and possible inventions) and refers to the basics for an early computer. It isn't clear if they actually built such a machine, but the theory and plans for one are there. The book was commissioned for the Caliph of Baghdad, who may have had one at least partially constructed. There is also reference to a Babylonian computer (which may have been used for defense purposes) given by the scientist Abu Rayhan al-Biruni (973–1048) around AD 1000. He describes a highly complex mechanism with many gears, which may have been used to calculate the movement of the planets—to determine time—and perhaps the movement and deployment of troops.

So widespread were these reports of ancient mechanisms that some of them were incorporated into legends coming out of the Middle and Far East. Thus, the Chinese Chi-Yu may have been some sort of vehicle powered by one of these early computers. And indeed some of the early "dragons" of Chinese and Eastern mythology *might* have been similar vehicles. In certain tales there are descriptions of a great "wing," which the creature lowered to one side of its massive body—this might conceivably be a loading ramp that might have been used to take on men and equipment. The legends also seem to suggest that the "dragon" also had great "whiskers," which may suggest some sort of antennae used for guidance. However, these are only suggestions.

It was not only powerful computers that were to be found in the ancient world—automata and robots existed there too. There has already been mention made of the Stoic academy in Rhodes, which may have produced the Antikytherea Mechanism. However, the academy is thought to have produced much more. There are stories of toys and small humanoid

figures that were able to move of their own accord created by the mathematicians and inventors for their own amusement and that of others. The Greek lyric poet Pindar (522–443 BC), states in one of his verses:

The automated figures stand
Adorning every public street,
And seem to breathe in stone or
Move their marble feet.

This was taken to be a description of the cities of Rhodes, but later scholars think that Pindar was actually talking about the city of Corinth in Sicily, which may imply a connection with Archimedes. Whether this was an exaggeration or not is unclear, but the idea of "moveable statues" and "automated images" clearly exercised the ancient mind. And there seems to have been a widespread idea that automated mechanisms were placed in the statues of certain gods and goddesses all across the Greek and Roman worlds in order to give them the appearance of life and to awe their worshippers. Whether this was true or not is uncertain, but the idea seems to have been a relatively common one. Certain traditions also gave these images mechanized voices—legend stated that the alleged ancient Athenian inventor Daedalus (who may not have existed) constructed a mechanized woman with a voice that he had created by inducing quicksilver into her workings. Jewish tradition also said that King Solomon made himself a mechanised throne carved with animals and human figures, which hailed him as monarch when he sat upon it. Even more wonderful, an eagle placed a crown on his head as soon as he was seated and a mechanized dove flew down to bring him a scroll from the Torah. Although there may be no actual truth in many of these stories there certainly *were* automated devices in these early times.

The inventor and mathematician Heros (sometimes rendered as Heron) of Alexandria (AD 10–70) created a number of programmed devices that included a vehicle (possibly a cart) that could move by itself along a predetermined route. It may even have used an early form of computer that had been built into it. Heros is further credited with creating an *aeropile* (a steam engine—one of the first recorded in the world), which powered a number of his inventions, some of which may have included humanoid figures. Indeed, the idea of the ancient computers and automatons became linked in the ancient mind, and legends suggest that scholars such as Archimedes were commissioned to design a series of robotic "soldiers" to defend some of the cities and ports of the classical Mediterranean world and some areas further East. Whether these were ever built or not is problematical, but designs for them may exist.

During the Northern Qi Dynasty (AD 550–577) in China, for instance, it was said that Emperor Wu Cheng commanded one of two major inventors—either King Lan Ling or Ling Zhao—to construct a robot army for him in order to defeat barbarian groups that were attacking his provinces. (King Lan Ling had already built an automaton for the emperor—a being that appeared to be of non-Chinese ethnicity, which danced and sang "in a reedy voice" for the Imperial court). There is, however, no record if this army of mechanical soldiers was ever built. We do know from accounts written at the time that the emperor had a small motorized boat—probably driven by some sort of steam engine—in which he carried goblets and carafes of wine across an ornamental lake to where he was sitting in the shade.

There is also an account that an inventor (and local magistrate) named Yin Winling from Louzhou Province in China built two wooden figures for the emperor. One was of a tiny wooden man who was placed on a small podium at the start of each banquet and mechanically raised a glass and proposed a toast to the emperor's health. If guests did not drink enough wine, the wooden man refilled their goblets while a small wooden girl appeared and sang, encouraging them to drink more. No one was able to ascertain how these automatons worked, but it is thought that they were guided by an early form of computer. Yet another inventor, Yang Wulain, created a wooden monk, which stood at the corner of a street in the city where he lived (Quingzhou City in Shandong Province, Eastern China), holding out a begging bowl in which passersby could deposit money. When the bowl was filled, the "monk" shook it slightly, bowed, and intoned "Alms solicited" in a thin mechanized voice. So many people wanted to hear it speak that its bowl soon filled up with several thousand wen (the coin of the lowest denomination—so although extremely popular it didn't make much money). No one knew how Yang Wulain had made the effigy move or the source of the voice, but some sort of mechanism must have existed.

In the Middle East, the idea of creating programmable robots continued. Perhaps the greatest of all creators of such automata was the mysterious al-Jazari (AD 1136–1206) who came from an area of Mesopotamia (now part of Iraq). Not much is known about this rather enigmatic character except that he left behind a wonderful book that became something of an inspiration to many later European inventors—the *Kitab fi-Ma'rifat al-Hiyal-Handasiyya* (Book of Knowledge of Ingenious Mechanical Devices). Among the devices explored would appear to be the framework for a mechanical musical band, which Al-Jazari actually created. Among his many other inventions—he lists more than 50 in the *Kitab*—are a crankshaft, a flush toilet, a process for the lamination of timber to prevent warping, and a combination lock for a trunk, safe, or door. Al-Jazari was also a pioneer in the use of hydraulics and is supposed to have created a mechanical man who moved and ran using these principles. And yet he remains a figure of mystery—his name is given as Abyu al-iz Ismail-al-Razaz al Jazari—part of his name simply refers to an area of northern Mesopotamia. He was probably attached to the court of Nasar al-Din, an Urtuq ruler of Diyor Bikr in Anatolian Turkey, for whom he is said to have constructed a series of wonderful water-clocks. He also seems to have left a number of designs for automatons, which passed through many hands throughout the Middle Ages. Some of these are supposed to have influenced later medieval inventors such as Roger Bacon.

Indeed, similar to the alchemists it is the early Middle Eastern and Far Eastern texts that influenced European medieval thinking and invention. It is even said that the great Italian artist and inventor Leonardo da Vinci (1452–1519) may have taken some of the early Islamic designs and incorporated them in some of his inventive plans. In 1515, da Vinci is known to have made a mechanical lion for King Francis I of France (who became a close personal friend), which could walk forward and then open its chest to reveal a cluster of lilies, the symbol of the French monarchy. In his later years, da Vinci also produced a programmable steam cannon and wrote his famed *Codex on the Flights of Birds* while designing an aerial screw helicopter. Some of the inventions that he described may have been based (in part at least) on early texts from what became widely known as The Golden Age of Islam. Da Vinci aside, many of the devices that were produced in Europe during medieval times were not as technologically advanced as those that were produced in earlier eras. Part of the reason for this may well have been the attitude of the Christian Church, which viewed the creation of such things as an affront against God (particularly if they were researched from Islamic texts), and so many of the early European inventors had to conduct experiments in relative secrecy, lacking the status, materials, and patronage (which was essential in these times) to develop their work. And many of the learned men in Europe were often connected to the Church in some way—whether they be monks, friars, bishops, or scholars (who studied and taught at monasteries and at Church-maintained schools—practically the only way of receiving an education during the early medieval period). There were, however, some churchmen who managed to take their studies into more "experimental" avenues including, it is said, the invention of mechanical men.

One of these was the Dominican Bishop Albert of Cologne (born somewhere between 1193 and 1206 and died in 1280), a churchman greatly interested in mathematics. He would, however, become better known for his explorations in more esoteric fields as Albertus Magnus (Great Albert). As an intellectual, there were many scientific avenues that interested Albert. Although he expounded upon the works of Aristotle, he was also deeply interested in astrology. It was also whispered that he was interested in alchemy and that he may even have discovered the Philosopher's Stone—although this is simply legend. A number of books are also attributed to him—the *Secreti Alberti* and *Experimenta Alberti* and at least one grimoire. All of these are probably spurious and were probably not written by the bishop at all, but by later persons. Other accounts of him, however, claim that he was also a celebrated inventor who secretly translated a number of early Islamic texts concerning mechanics.

He was allegedly asked by the Church to construct a man of brass who would act as its defender. The Church itself was coming under increasing attack from within its own ranks. Having confidently predicted the End of the World and Christ's return by the year AD 1000 it now looked increasingly precarious when that event did not happen. Added to this, a number of orders of monks were under attack by a number of minor writers such as William of Saint-Armour (1200–1272) who were stirring passions by denouncing certain religions as heretical. The Church (and the orders) was fearful that such writings could incite popular uprisings in certain parts of Europe. Consequently many monastic houses, especially the Dominicans (one of the central orders of the Holy Inquisition), felt the need to physically protect themselves from a possible social upheaval, and this may have been the reason behind the request to Albert. It is said that the bishop (he was then Bishop of Regensburg in Germany, having been elevated to that position by Pope Alexander IV), using ancient Islamic texts, created a man of brass that could be programmed to fight if need be. By this time, the times had changed a little and the Church perceived that the threat of social unrest had receded slightly, so the brass man was used as a servant instead. The robot manservant continued with Albert until his death, and he bequeathed it (together, say some, with the Philosopher's Stone) to one of his students, St. Thomas Aquinas, who took great exception to the gift and had the brass man (and the Stone) destroyed. Perhaps he considered the robot too dangerous to have around at such an unsettled time. Maybe he thought that its creation was an affront against God, who was deemed to have sole authority over the creation of life. Bishop Albert was beatified by Pope Gregory XV in 1622 and was later canonized as a Doctor of the Church by Pope Pius XI in 1931, and yet the taint of witchcraft and strange inventions still hung over him. The notion of the man of brass may not have completely disappeared, as Albertus Magnus was one of the writers whom Mary Shelley cited as having been read by Victor Frankenstein while studying the occult.

Roger Bacon

Besides Albertus, another great philosopher and alleged alchemist and inventor was the English 13th-century Franciscan friar Roger Bacon. A controversial figure throughout his life, Bacon (like Albertus and many other academics of his day) was a follower and student of Aristotle, whose texts written in poor Greek only existed in England. Bacon applied himself to studying languages and in the process acquired a number of ancient Islamic texts. He is also known to have corresponded with a certain Petrus Pereginus of Picardy (possibly Pierre Perelini de Maricourt, who lived around 1269 and was a noted French mathematician whose speciality was magnetism). Very little is known about this individual except that, in 1269, he may have been part of the army of Charles Duc d'Anjou that laid siege to the city of Lucera in the Apulia area of southern Italy which was held at the time by Sicilian Muslims. It is therefore thought that this Petrus may have been a soldier or a Crusader, although the name "Pereginus" suggests that he may have been a holy pilgrim and may well have taken part in the siege under directions from the pope. But nobody is really sure. Whoever he was, he was a skilled mathematician and was greatly admired by Bacon.

Among their correspondence were said to have been detailed plans for a "fighting man made of brass or metal," which Petrus had been asked to design for the duc. This appears to have been some sort of programmable fighting robot, which might have been used against enemies such as the Moors or Saracens who were fighting in parts of Spain and in the Holy Land. It might also have been a mechanized suit of armor, which could be worn like a garment. Within this correspondence, it was said, were exact details of how the mechanism would operate (supposedly on a system of hydraulics) and how it might be programmed. It was said that this was the origin of the brass head that is referred to at the start of this chapter, or perhaps Bacon actually built the robot/robotic suit. If he did there is no real record of this except from legend. Or if Petrus built the device in southern Italy there is also no official record. But the legend that Roger Bacon had built *something* still persisted.

Bacon wrote a number of works, most of which he sent to Pope Clement IV. In 1267, he sent his major work, appropriately entitled *Opus Majus* (Greater Work), which outlined a whole number of ideas, many taken and developed from earlier Islamic texts. Included in it was a discussion on hydraulics and how this might be included in certain devices. The following year, 1268, Bacon further sent the pope a summary of the work entitled *Opus Minus.* What is interesting about this correspondence (and perhaps explains it) is that Clement was a rather controversial pontiff, having formerly been a married soldier with two daughters, who maintained an interest in all things military. Included in the text that Bacon sent were a number of military elements including the recipe for the making of gunpowder (the introduction of which into Western Europe is generally ascribed to Roger Bacon). It is not known whether Clement took great cognizance of the literature (perhaps he did), but certainly subsequent generations appear to have, according Bacon the status of a miraculous inventor and entwining his name with legend.

Roger Bacon is also credited (perhaps erroneously) as being an author of the so-called Voynich Manuscript. This mysterious book, which takes its name from the Polish-American book dealer, Wilfred M. Voynich, who acquired it in 1912, was supposedly written in the 15th or 16th centuries and in a language or intricate cipher that none can understand. It also contains many elaborate drawings of stars, planets, indefinable spheres, animals, and plants, and is said to contain secrets that are now lost to the modern world. The volume has defied translation (both American and British code-breakers were brought in to translate the work during World War II—all of them failed). It is said that included in the indecipherable text may be instructions on how to either "grow" beings or else create them from metals. No one, however, is certain. Nor is anyone sure who penned the book (the text is handwritten); for many Roger Bacon remains one of the prime contenders. The untranslated manuscript is now in the Beinecke Rare Book and Manuscript Library of Yale University.

Ambroise Paré

Aside from full-bodied automata, during the 15th and 16th centuries, mechanical devices were also being considered as replacements for body parts that had been lost. An increase of warfare across Europe led to a number of arms and legs being amputated, lopped off, or blown off, either by gunpowder or by accident. If these parts could be replaced by a mechanism, it was suggested, soldiers could continue fighting, perhaps with increased strength, thus creating what might be counted as early cyborg warriors. One of the foremost in such thinking was the French physician Ambroise Paré (born in either 1510 or 1517), who acted as chief Royal Surgeon for four French monarchs—Henry II, Francis II, Charles IX, and Henry III. As the Wars of Religion began to take hold all across France, so the instances of those presenting themselves with serious wounds and loss of limb increased immeasurably, and as a forerunner in battlefield surgery,

Paré began to consider how a partly mechanized soldier might be created. His intentions were certainly good, but he had to be careful. The French churches, both Catholic and Protestant, both held that the body was the creation of God and that Man should not tamper with it, no matter what befell it. Paré certainly enjoyed both the patronage and protection of the monarchy, but he had to tread warily.

Nevertheless in 1574/5, he published a medical work entitled *Les Oeuvres de Ambroise Paré* based (it is said) on his experiences with the French army in Northern Italy, which contained a design for a "gripper" or iron hand with flexible fingers. This was supposed to be attached by straps to an amputated arm and used pretty much as an ordinary hand. The device was a sophisticated one, having sprockets attached to each finger with a mechanized shaft going through them on which they could turn, a trigger to hold each finger with a button on the end of each to flex them and open the hand, and springs on each one to make them go back and to hold the hand in a closed fist. There were several other modifications, such as flexible blades on the fingers and thumb making the entire device not too different from prosthetic limbs, which were to come later.

Perhaps because of the devices that he was working on, Paré was denounced by the Catholic Church (it might also have been because he was a French Protestant), and during upheavals in Paris following the Massacre of the Innocents (August 24, 1572), had to be locked in a clothes cupboard by Charles IX in order to hide. He died in Paris in 1590 leaving behind a wealth of mechanical devices (many of which were designed for amputees), which were said to have been destroyed on the orders of the Church. (By now France was a formally Catholic country following the conversion to the faith of Henry IV in 1589.)

Paré may have been influenced slightly by a new fad that was sweeping Europe. From the mid-1500s, groups of entertainers were visiting cities, towns, and villages with a show of "animated dolls." These were tiny metal dancing figures that were powered by internal mechanisms, which performed in many streets and squares all across the Continent. They were, it was said, built in the style of the earlier Chinese figures (known as "kar-akuri-ningyo"), which had graced the palaces of the Emperors and noble-men there. In Europe they performed short plays and acted very much as animated puppets to the delight of many audiences. As such they became something of a fashion, especially in parts of France where they were to be seen as late as the 18th century.

Jacques de Vaucanson

They may indeed have inspired another Frenchman, Jacques de Vaucanson, who had been born in Grenoble in 1709. (It is worth noting that he was simply born as Jacques Vaucanson, the son of a poor glove-maker; the "de" was later added by the Academie de Sciences). Like many of his prede-cessors, de Vaucanson was something of a mathematical genius, but he was highly interested in mechanical science and planned to become a clock-maker. However, he was also deeply religious, and after a Jesuit schooling, he joined a religious order in Lyon (the Minims, which flourished in France at the time) with the intention of becoming a priest. An accidental meeting with the great surgeon Claud-Nicolas Le Chat (1700–1768) sparked his interest in mechanical devices once more and also gave him an interest in anatomy, and he left the order to pursue his studies in that direction

At the age of only 18 he received the patronage of a prominent noble-man who gave him a workshop in Lyon. His benefactor asked him to make a series of machines that would be useful around the house, and Vaucanson obliged. He may have also seen some of the animated performing dolls in the streets around Lyon, which probably intrigued him. Hearing of their former brother's great successes, the Minims decided to pay him a visit, and in 1727, the local head of the order together with some government of-ficials invited themselves for a meal. In order to impress them, Vaucanson decided to build some automatons, which would wait the table and supply them with wine. The move proved to be a disaster, for although the automatons were excellent and behaved perfectly the religious leader declared the inventions "profane" and an insult to God, and instructed the officials to destroy his workshop. However, they were unable to stop Vaucanson from creating more mechanical figures. His knowledge of anatomy had ensured that his machines functioned very much like ordinary men, mimicking human activities such as circulation and respiration. Throughout the years, he had refined his techniques and had created almost perfect androids and he was determined to develop his skills further, no matter what the Church thought.

In 1737 Vaucanson made one of his most famous creations: The Flute Player. This was a full-size figure of a young shepherd playing a pipe, which had a repertoire of 12 melodies. The fingers of the figure actually moved, but very stiffly, so Vaucanson procured a large envelope of skin to cover his work and enable them to move more smoothly. The result was presented to the *Academie des Sciences* in 1738. The automaton created a sensation. Although France was well used to metal toys, this was something far more sophisticated and it earned its inventor great prestige, despite the denouncements of the Church. Vaucanson quickly followed it up with two other automatons—The Tambourine Player and The Digesting Duck (the latter is considered a true masterpiece of mechanical engineering). The duck was able to flap its wings, drink water, eat corn, and "defecate" (the corn was held in one section of its "stomach" and droppings were held in another that were released by a spring mechanism). However, the design for the digestive system was completely accurate and was based on Vaucanson's knowledge of anatomy. He is also credited as having developed the world's first rubber tube in order to make the "digestion" more effective. Although he gained great credit for his inventions Vaucanson grew weary of them quite quickly and sold them off.

The skill of his inventions, however, brought him to the attention of Frederick II of Prussia, who offered to be his patron and to install him at the Prussian Court. Although the offer was tempting, Vaucanson refused, declaring himself to be a "Frenchman through and through." He declared that he would only work for French patrons. And indeed, he was rewarded in his own country. In 1741, he was approached by Cardinal Fleury, Minister of State for King Louis XV of France and appointed as inspector for the country's manufacture of silk. He was to oversee and advise upon the making of silk products all across the country (which had fallen behind the standards of England, Ireland, and Scotland). In his new role, Vaucanson promoted new methods for the spinning of silk thread, including designing the first completely automated loom. He also began to work on computerized punch cards, such as those that would be used in the early 20th century, but never completed the project. (His work would later be refined by Joseph-Marie Jacquard [1752–1834] who would revolutionize the French spinning industry with the Jacquard loom.)

It is said that when he had time, Vaucanson continued to make automatons, although largely for his own amusement and the amazement of his friends. There are also suggestions that he was approached by the French Department for War regarding the possibility of making computerized automatons, which might be used in battle. It is said that he submitted some designs, but what became of them is unknown—were such soldiers secretly developed by the French? However, in 1746, de Vaucanson was made a formal Member of the Academie des Sciences. He died in Paris in 1782, bequeathing most of his inventions and his large library of designs to the French king, Louis XVI, and this would become the basis of the Conservatoire des Artes et Metiers in Paris. However, many of his marvelous inventions, including the Flute Player, were said to have been destroyed during the French Revolution in 1789 when many of his designs were also burned. He had, however, left a legacy of ideas regarding the viability of automatons in general life and in possible military action.

Friedrich Kauffmann

Inspired perhaps by Vaucanson's work, a German inventor from Dresden, Friedrich Kauffmann (1785–1866), created a trumpet-playing military-style figure, which was about as tall as a full-grown man. The figure was both imposing and threatening, although the "music" that it made was said to be poor. Its repertoire was rather limited and the sound was of a feeble quality. Nevertheless, it looked very much the military man, and indeed many people who saw it were frightened by it. The trumpeter is currently housed in the Deutches Museum in Munich. Such formidable-looking automatons reflect the thinking of the time, which was gradually moving toward a "reinvention" of the mechanical warriors of classical legend; now they were adopting a more sinister and monstrous aspect.

Pierre Jacquet-Droz

Kauffmann, of course, wasn't the only inventor working in the field of menacing automata. In 1772 a Swiss watchmaker, Pierre Jacquet-Droz (1721–1790) and his son Henri-Louis (1746–1866) had created an android that could actually write. The "robot" was in the form of a small boy seated at a desk that could write a few simple, preprogrammed sentences onto a page in front of it. It was composed of more than 600 parts, and is generally regarded as an early form of computer. It was so lifelike that people were at pains to tell it from a real child, and once more were rather frightened of it. Pierre Jacquet-Droz then created an even more complicated mechanical tableau, which was presented to the visiting king of Spain (the inventions had attracted the attention of visiting heads of state from all over Europe, China, and India). The display consisted of a clock in which an African-American servant spoke the time while a shepherd played a series of tunes in the background and a dog approached and nuzzled him. Jacquet-Droz then asked the king to offer the dog an apple, which he did, and the mechanism barked so loudly that the monarch's own dog responded in kind. The Catholic courtiers were terrified, and, suspecting witchcraft, crossed themselves and tried to withdraw. The king, however, asked his minister to enquire the time from the African-American servant, but gave the mechanism gave no reply. Jacquet-Droz quickly observed that the mechanism had not had the time to learn Spanish.

These mechanisms were so lifelike and complex that, although a wonder to the aristocracy, were beginning to incite fear among the serving and lower classes. They were now being looked at as mechanical monsters, and there was the start of a widespread fear that they might one day become so complicated that they would turn upon their masters and overthrow the human race. The idea of a monstrous army of automatons was already being born in the common mind.

Other Stories

There was little doubt that the idea of a mechanized man had now entered the public consciousness in a big way, and was being reflected by popular culture. They were already being written about in adventure stories for teenage boys. One of the earliest writers in the genre was Edward S. Ellis (1840–1916), who, well before the development of steampunk, wrote of another "steaming" character, *The Steam Man of the Prairies,* now widely regarded as the first science-fiction dime novel. This was largely an action novel in the style of James Fenimore Cooper (whom Ellis admired) and dealt with a great steam-powered robotic man fighting Red Indians and overcoming natural disasters. It was hugely popular, first appearing in *Beadle's American Novels* (No 45, August 1868), and then being reprinted no less than six times throughout the years—something akin to a science-fiction best-seller. It also paved the way for another adventure series featuring robots—the Frank Reade stories. These, too, were adventure tales and used the concepts that Ellis had developed. The first was written by Harry Enton and was entitled *Frank Reade and his Steam Man of the Plains* (seemingly a direct connection to Ellis's work). The stories appeared in the juvenile fiction series Boys of New York during February to April 1876 and were high-action tales primarily based around inventions, most of which were steam-powered robots.

Having created a market and an interest, a long series of similar novels were published by Irwin's American Novels, which featured the son of the inventor Frank Reade—Frank Reade, Jr. These were also aimed at adolescent boys and were written by the reasonably celebrated writer Luis P. Senarens (1865–1939), but using the pseudonym "Noname" to disguise who he was. Under his authorship there was a Stem Man Mark II and a Mark III, and later an Electric Man as well. Once again, the series was immensely popular and spawned a number of imitators and similar themes. The idea of steam and mechanical robots were now included in what was to become known as "invention fiction." But such stories were also establishing the robot—whether it was powered by steam or an internal mechanism—as a huge and monstrous figure, which might run amok and threaten those around it at any time.

There was another element in thinking about machines as well. In 1822, a British inventor named Charles Babbage had invented what he called a "Difference Engine." In all actuality this was something of an extension of Jacquard's automated loom. Jacquard had planned a series of slotted punch cards in order to activate and power the looms he designed, but had never really brought this plan to fruition. A skilled mathematician, Babbage (1791–1871) developed the same cards to slot into and power functions of the engine, which was in fact a giant calculating machine. (The term *computer* was already in use in Babbage's day, but it specifically referred to human beings—those who "computed" calculations and equations. The human process was, inevitably, widely open to continual error.) Using a system of finite differences (methods for the numerical solution of differential equations and value problems) Babbage used his engine to calculate without really using multiplication, addition, or division. The machine stood 8 feet tall and weighed 15 tons, and for 1822 when it was built, it was one of the most complicated devices of its day. It was, in effect, an early computer (Babbage is credited as being the "father of the modern computer"), and was supposedly more accurate in its deliberations than many of our calculators today. But once again, it was rather menacing and unwieldy. Babbage designed a "Difference Engine Mark II," but this was never built during his lifetime—in fact it was not built and put in action until 1989-1991.

What Babbage had created was a "thinking machine," and this was swiftly linked to the idea of automatons in the general mind. If complex machines like Babbage's computer could think for themselves then so could automated warriors. The idea of the monstrous machine, specifically designed to help man but ultimately turning on him, began to resurface again (if it had ever gone away). The word *robot* was not used, but it would be in 1921 in a play by the Czech writer Karel Capek entitled *R.U.R.* (Rosum's Universal Robots). Capek always credited his brother Josef, an artist, with the "invention" of the word (*robota*) with relation to metal beings. Originally, the word was similar to the German *arbeiter* meaning a life of mindless drudgery, and was used in the Czech tongue to denote serfdom and servitude. Capek had originally intended to call the automatons in his fictional work *labori* (meaning "labor"), but thought it sounded "too book-ish" and, on his brother's advice, opted for the word *roboti* instead. In the public mind he created a thinking robotic serving class, which had been created to serve Mankind but, like their human counterparts, and as history had shown, might one day rise up and overthrow human institutions. Indeed, Capek's play suggested the end of the human race at the metallic hands of the automatons. The menace of the monstrous thinking machine had now entered human perception and it was probably worse than anything that had gone before, as it signaled the very end of all human things. And what seemed even more monstrous was the fact that those human beings had actually *built* the machines, and so were, in effect, the authors of their own destruction.

Capek's idea of menacing robots, whether individual or as a rampaging group, continued throughout the years and dominated the plots of many science-fiction books and films. Humanity, it appeared, seemed to be continually waging a war against the advancing machines, whether it be in the present, the far future, or on some distant planet similar to our own. Images of the looming, menacing robots have assailed us in both television and film, from the hulking Gort in Robert Wise's celebrated 1951 classic *The Day the Earth Stood Still* (based on the short story by Harry Bates entitled *Farewell to the Master*), through the out-of-control androids in Michael Crichton's *Westworld* (1973), to the menacing machines of the Terminator series, culminating in *Terminator Salvation* (2009). All of these films have contained an underlying menace from the machines, which has become deeply rooted in the public psyche throughout the years.

It was not a great intellectual step from the building of a man of metal to the creation by artificial means of a being of flesh and blood. After the robot, the clone (a living, identical replicant made from the genetic material of an existing being and with the same genetic code) seemed to be the next logical thing to do. And in a sense, cloning has already been occurring in the natural world for thousands of years. A number of trees and plants are self-pollinating and share exactly the same genetic code. A large forest, for example, might have been created from just one tree with new plants growing from the roots of just one growth. This, however, is natural cloning, and there was no attempt at any artificial method until the 19th century.

Cloning

In the 1890s, a German biologist from Bad Kreuznach in the Rhineland named Hans Adolf Driesch began a series of experiments deigned to split the large embryos of sea urchins. It needs to be stressed that he was not seeking to make a clone, but was trying to determine what happened to

the genetic material when the embryo was split. In doing so, he created a population of identical sea urchins, which might be considered as the first real clones.

His work may have served to inspire another German biological scientist from Stuttgart, Hans Spemann (1869–1941), who is often referred to as "the father of cloning." Around 1902, he experimented with splitting salamander cells, using a hair from the head of his infant son to cut them in two. Like Dreisch before him, he was determined to prove that cell-splitting did not result in the loss of genetic material as had been previously argued. By splitting the cell into two, he successfully produced two larvae that grew into two salamanders. His cell research won Spenmann the Nobel Prize for Science, but there were many who worried where his research was taking Mankind.

Although Spemann and Dreisch had not deliberately set out to create life, there were many objections to the work. The first was a moral one: Even though the scientific age was beginning to dawn, there was still a distinct feeling that the creation of life—albeit accidental—was the province of God alone. In medieval times, alchemists had claimed to have "grown" being-like plants from "seeds" in their alembics, prompting the Church to denounce them as heretics (indeed in response the pope had specifically issued a Bull condemning the practice of alchemy), and something of that idea still persisted even into the early years of the 20th century. Even the accidental artificial creation of life was still viewed as a usurpation of the Divine prerogative. Men had no business tinkering with a function that more properly belonged to God, for who knew where it would lead—the birth of monsters, perhaps? It was not right that each created being should be exactly the same, as God had differentiated between us all for a specific purpose.

The second objection was born out of a deep-seated fear: If metal automatons might overthrow Mankind, so might an army of clones. Once again the path that such scientific development led toward might mean the destruction of all true human beings. Indeed these "clones" were even more terrifying, as they were like humans themselves and, not being machines, could not be disconnected or deprogrammed. So strong were these objections that for a time all research into genetic development remained largely in abeyance. It continued to do so for the early part of the 20th century. But the imperative to experiment with genetics nevertheless still lay somewhere deep in the scientific mind.

In 1951 a group of American scientists in Philadelphia under the direction of Professor Robert W. Briggs began an experiment with frogs' eggs. This was not an attempt to separate the genetic material of the egg, but rather to modify it. They removed the nucleus from the unfertilized nucleus of the egg's embryo cell and replaced it with the fertilised nucleus from another one, and they produced new frogs. This basic action known as a "nuclear transplant" is still (with a number of modifications) used in genetics today. Even though the experiment was a success, it provoked a great deal of opposition and outrage during the early 1950s—Briggs and his team had been deliberately trying to create life—and there were questions as to whether this procedure might be allowed in future. The implications were that life might very well be created in human cells.

In the 1970s, however, there were rumors of other cloning experiments in Germany. Mice were supposed to have been cloned by scientists and some details were supposedly released, although no results were really seen. Most scientists all across the world adjudged these reports to be a hoax, perpetrated in order to gain both fame and finance for the team involved. In one "demonstration" (in 1977) various mouse embryos were found in test tubes at different stages of development, certainly suggesting some form of "sleight of hand." And despite other claims the idea of cloning remained, for a number of years, firmly in the realm of science fiction.

The first real cloning breakthrough came in 1986 when teams of scientists on both sides of the Atlantic announced that they were on the verge of creating a cloned animal. The British team was led by Steen Willadsen, who announced that they were almost ready to produce a cloned sheep. In America, another team led by Neal First suggested they clone a cow. Neither team was successful, but from their efforts much was learned about cloning techniques and about developing embryos under laboratory conditions. Their work served both as an inspiration and as a scientific base for those who came after them.

In 1986 Ian Wilmut of the Roslin Institute in Scotland was given a brief based on Willadsen's work. The brief was to clone a sheep that produced a certain type of chemical in its milk. Part of the work had, of course, already been done, and so Wilmut commenced the paperwork in 1987 and was ready to begin the procedure in 1990. Wilmut theorized that by starving the cells, he could force them into a GO phase, similar to hibernation, which would increase their chances of survival. The theory worked, and in 1996, he successfully cloned a lamb from the mammary cells of another sheep, and, being a big country and western fan, he named it Dolly after the singer Dolly Parton. Dolly was not perfect, and was subject to a number of illnesses, such as progressive lung diseases and severe arthritis. She was, however, successfully bred on a Welsh mountain ram and produced a number of lambs. Later, her illnesses, especially the arthritis, became steadily worse, and although she was treated with anti-inflammatory drugs, in the end she found it difficult to actually walk. At last, in 2003, she developed a lung infection that became a cancer, causing her death. Although she could have lived for more than 11 or 12 years, she died when she was 6, and it has been postulated that she was born at around the same genetic age as the animal from which she was cloned. However, scientists have argued that the disease developed from being extensively kept indoors (she spent all her life in the Roslin Institute) and not through imperfections in the cloning technique. Nevertheless, Dolly the Sheep rightly has the distinction of being the first completely cloned animal in history. Since then, there have been a number of mammals cloned in various laboratories in England, America, and Southeast Asia, to much shock and dismay among religious groupings in all three countries. Sheep, bulls, and other animals (some endangered species) have been successfully cloned in the East and there have been other experiments carried out in Europe with positive results. There is even some rumor that in 2008, a process was begun in the United States that might be able to clone a living human being, and although severe limitations were placed upon the research by the administration of President George W. Bush, it is said that a number of experiments in that field have already been carried out. However, no data on the matter has yet emerged, and the stories remain in the area of scientific speculation. Some-where in America, runs the argument, there is a secret government base in which experiments are carried out to produce, through genetic cloning manipulation, a soldier who has no fear and who can't feel pain, to use in battlefields such as Afghanistan and Iraq. However, this is merely speculation and conspiracy theory.

To some extent, the clone has replaced the robot as the created monster lurking somewhere in the shadows, waiting to strike. The idea of a partly human army created in some distant laboratory, moving to usurp our posi-tion in the world, is indeed a frightening prospect. It is a long way from the ancient men of brass, guided by antique mechanisms protecting island states or defending autonomous cities, to the modern nightmare of robot legions or squads of men perhaps created in vats, threatening humanity and guided by computers. This premise has indeed formed the basis of countless science-fiction books, television series, and films. Although our fear of alchemical goblins lurking in jars might now be discounted, under-neath all our so-called sophistication the fear is the same—of what man can do, of what he might just be able to create. Frankenstein is certainly alive and well and living in the 21st century.

CONCLUSION

RETURN TO THE DUST

FOR YOU ARE OF DUST AND TO DUST YOU SHALL RETURN.

—GENESIS 3:19

IN 1974, SOME WORKMEN were digging near the city of Xi'an in the Shaanxi Province of northwestern China when they made a strange and alarming discovery. Xi'an is one of China's oldest cities—one of the country's four ancient capitals—and is considered a center of culture in the area. The workmen unearthed pieces of metal and terracotta, but suddenly part of the ground caved in and they found themselves looking into some sort of pit. As they investigated further, peering into the gloom of the hole, they found an immobile humanoid face looking back at them, sending them running for the authorities. What was later unearthed has proved to be one of the wonders of both the ancient and modern worlds—it was an army lying in wait, guarding the entrance to a huge underground necropolis. This is the famous terracotta army of Qin Shi Huang, China's first emperor.

In the third century BC China was slowly pulling itself together from quarrelling dominions into a formal empire. It was also under increasing attack from barbarians based in the north and west. In the midst of the confusion, a young nobleman named Yin Zheng seized power and began to pull the feuding forces into a cohesive entity. He styled himself Qin Shi Huang (literally "First Emperor"), and would found a regime that would last during his lifetime, a period of almost 20 years (the Qin Dynasty, 221–206 BC) and which would stabilize the greater part of China, bringing an end to what has become known as the Era of Warring States. Claiming that he was guided by a vision, he invaded neighboring territories where the older Chu and Zhu Dynasties held sway, subjugating them and adding them to his own province. He would also lay the foundations of the Great Wall of China to keep out marauding barbarian hordes.

Although he certainly had an over-inflated ego, Qin Shi Huang was deeply superstitious and was terrified of dying. He imagined that on the point of death his spirit would be seized by demons and taken away to some awful hell where he would be subjected to eternal torment. He became obsessed with immortality and on the advice of (perhaps fraudulent) physicians, he continually took mercury tablets in attempt to extend his lifespan (in all actuality these probably killed him). Not only this, but he decided to build a vast underground necropolis—a funeral city—where his body could lie in peace unmolested by the demons, which he imagined roamed the world outside. The task was a mammoth one, requiring a workforce of 720,000 people, engaged in carving out a great underground cavern, complete with burial pits, and in constructing a vast city together with a central palace for the emperor. It took 37 years to build. Indeed, the city was at the center of a vast underground kingdom over which Qin Shi Huang would rule in death as he had in life. Nevertheless, he was still terrified that demons or barbarians would attack him even after death, and was convinced that he needed to be protected. To do this, he constructed a "magic army" made up of life-size terracotta figures—8,000 soldiers, 130 chariots, 520 horses, and 150 cavalry horses have so far been uncovered—in order to guard both himself and his dead kingdom. Although scientists know the numbers that make up the "army" of figures, many of these have not really been excavated, but still lie in burial pits. Scientists estimate that there may be as many as 6,000 more under the earth, awaiting discovery.

Even though the figures had no living existence in this world, they were supposed to have a spiritual counterpart in the Otherworld where demons and ghosts that might menace the emperor dwelt. And they are supposed to have been facially modeled on some of the emperor's own guards. Not only were there soldiers and horses, but there were also tumblers, acrobats, and entertainers among the terracotta throng, presumably to amuse and divert Qin Shi Huang in his otherwise bleak underground country. For much of the information concerning the great city, scholars have had to rely on the works of the Chinese historian Sima Qian (145–90 BC), who wrote almost 100 years after the death of the Qin Emperor. He states that when Qin Shi Huang died in 210 BC he was laid to rest in the central palace of the underground city in a sealed tomb "with many wondrous objects." The emperor's tomb still remains sealed, as Sima states that it was surrounded by intricate defensive devices that were designed to kill tomb robbers—however, as he was prone to exaggeration, we must take what the historian says with a pinch of salt. Nevertheless there are bound to be many valuable artifacts within the tomb (just as there were in the tomb of Tutankhamen in Egypt), which the terracotta army has been placed to guard.

Since its discovery, the excavation of the necropolis has been slow (indeed for a number of years it had been stopped and has only just been restarted). One of the reasons given is that all work must be done carefully, in case some of the emperor's treasures might be damaged in the excavations (this happened with certain Egyptian tombs in the 1920s). Recently work recommenced on the Number 1 pit and yet more of the terracotta figures have been unearthed.

The reason for the construction of such a multitude of elaborate figures was ostensibly to protect the emperor in the Afterlife, but perhaps it was also thought that with the threat of barbarian invasion or a resumption of the Warring States, the terracotta "magic army" might protect him in a physical way as well. Using magic (in which Qin Shi Huang passionately believed) the army might be brought to life to defend the Qin regime. Furthermore, the emperor was a tyrant and was continually fearful of an insurrection against his authority. Again, the "magic army" could be used (although it never was) to put insurrectionists down and to maintain stability. The terracotta army, although seeming to be nothing more than curious figurines, might suddenly become a ravaging force that would defeat the emperor's enemies, whether military or supernatural. That, at least, was the belief behind such an elaborate construction. But, of course, there are other conflicting beliefs concerning these warriors.

There was a belief, for example (which might still be in vogue today in certain parts of China, and is sometimes given as the reason for the delay in opening the burial pits), that the terracotta soldiers might harbor demons that might one day turn on the populace. This may go back to the time of Qin Shi Huang who, as has already been stated, was widely regarded as something of a tyrant, who turned his soldiers on his own people almost without hesitation. The emperor thought that he was entitled to power and would apparently stop at nothing to hold on to it. Therefore, the army that was created by men for good—and for defense—might also become, under the influence of magic, something wholly evil.

And in a sense that premise is behind most types of man-made monsters. Many of the creatures that Mankind has supposedly created were not intended to do harm, but had the potential to do so (and usually finished up doing it). Whether it is out of scientific curiosity, for creating servants, or for making something with which to defend Humanity the potential for massive destruction is still the same. In many tales, both folktale and literary creation the creation ultimately turns upon its creators, thus becoming a monster.

This idea underpinned the perceptions concerning the creation of life in much of the ancient world—only the Creator (whether it be God or some other Supreme Being) was wise enough to bring into being the perfect, balanced individual. This was the teaching of many religions all across many former civilizations. If Mankind attempted to tinker with the process, they inevitably got it wrong and created something terrible and with awful consequences. Indeed, this idea still permeates at least part of our thinking today. Both experiments in robotics and cloning are met with some degree of horror and opposition here in the West, not only from Christian groups (who consider, just as in previous times, that the creation and modification of life is God's prerogative alone), but also of some others. Some, for example, consider that certain major governments are engaged in such processes to ultimately destroy democracy and civil liberties, and there are stories of "secret soldiers" being created in secluded governmental plants, such as in Area 51 in southern Nevada. Whether or not such theories are true is another matter. Others say that men are being cloned and modified to facilitate deep space exploration, but again no evidence is produced to uphold such a claim. And there are those who state that human genes are being crossed with those of animals to create a new species of human that

can survive in a world devastated by global warming, but that they haven't got the gene balance just right yet, and are creating monstrous, animalistic hybrids. Once again at present this is simply the stuff of science fiction. But there is often a genuine fear underlying such assertions.

Others are simply terrified as to where science will take us. Like Victor Frankenstein, will some "mad scientist" create a creature that will menace local communities or even the world? What, such people argue, lies ahead for us all in such an uncertain scientific future? In a rather obscure (but highly entertaining) movie made in 1941 by Universal Pictures and re-leased and re-released under a number of titles such as *Man-Made Monster, The Atomic Monster, The Human Robot*, and *The Electric Man,* Hollywood skillfully tapped into the Frankenstein idea of a creation out of control. The film, which saw the acting debut of Lon Chaney, Jr. (who would go on to star in such films as *The Wolf Man)* was directed by George Waggner and also starred Lionel Attwill as Dr. Paul Regas, a crazed scientist very much in the Frankenstein mold. The film was based on a short story called *The Electric Man*, which had been bought by Universal for $3,300, hoping to interest Boris Karloff and Bela Lugosi (neither of whom expressed any interest at all), and the screenplay by Harry Essex and Sid Schwartz had been languishing since the early 1930s before it was finally made into a movie. It suffered by being released under a number of titles, and because it was unfavorably compared with another more celebrated film *The Invisible Man*, which had been released slightly before it. Even so it strikingly reflected the fear that was already starting to permeate society regarding biological experiments in the 1940s and 1950s.

In the film, a bus is hit by an electric cable, the surge killing everybody on board except for gentle Dan McCormick (the part played by Chaney), who seems to be immune to electricity. This intrigues scientist Dr. John Lawrence who began to conduct some experiments on McCormick to see if a defense could be found against electric shock. However, Lawrence's rather evil assistant, Paul Regas, has other plans. He plans to create an army of electrobiogenic zombies that are under his personal control and sees McCormick's condition as a way of achieving this. Unbeknownst to Lawrence (whom he later accidentally kills) he continues secret experiments on the unfortunate man, giving controlled dosages of electricity until his mind gives way and he turns into a rampaging monster. McCormick now has the "touch of death" (electrocuting everyone whom he touches), and though Regas tries to control him, he finds that he can't. In the end McCormick goes wild, killing several people (including Regas) before finally running out of electricity and dying himself.

In spite of all its difficulties, the film proved reasonably popular and served in many respects to establish the idea of the "mad scientist" determined to create monsters by turning normal people into something else in the public consciousness. Some of these elements—a single scientist or group of scientists trying to achieve world domination through genetic manipulation (which then goes badly awry)—have continued throughout the years until even today.

And if man can create such a being then perhaps he might also destroy it—to send it back to the dust from which it was created. This is the underpinning legend of the Golem—the removal of the Word of Power or the clay tablet from its mouth. But the great fear may be that no means of destruction can be found or that the creation(s) will overwhelm Mankind before it can be achieved. And if that happens, then the time of natural humans will be past and man-made monsters will reign supreme.

The idea of Frankenstein or the Golem and other created creatures may perhaps be (superficially at least) consigned to the realm of Gothic literature and folklore, and yet the idea of the shrouded body on the scientist's laboratory slab or the movement in the alchemist's clouded jar still has the power to send a distinct chill of fear down all our spines. And as the pace of scientific research picks up at an alarming rate, and as science fiction sometimes merges with science fact, the creation of monstrous and terrifying beings becomes more and more of a possibility. Maybe somewhere close by, just around the corner, Frankenstein or some similar monster is waiting for us.

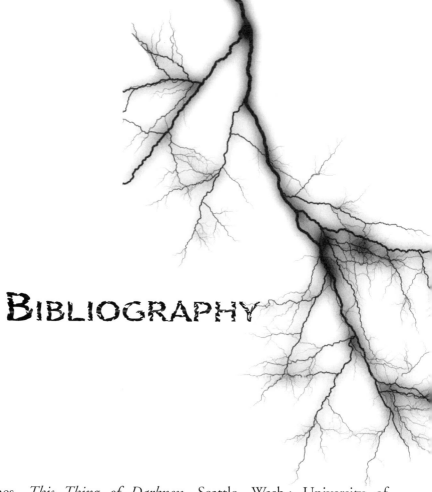

BIBLIOGRAPHY

Aho, James. *This Thing of Darkness*. Seattle, Wash.: University of Washington Press, 1994.

Aristotle. "On Marvellous Things Heard" in the *Complete Works of Aristotle*. Princeton, N.J.: Princeton University Press, 1995.

Arnikar, Hari Jeevan. *Essentials of Occult Chemistry and Modern Science*. Adyar, India: Theosophical Publishing House, 2000.

Beal, Timothy. *Religion and Its Monsters*. New York: Routledge, 2002.

Becker, Robert O. *Cross Currents: The Promise of Electromedicine, the Perils of Electropollution*. New York: Tarcher Putnam, 1990.

Becker, Robert O., and Gary Selden. *The Body Electric: Electromagnetism and the Foundation of Life*. New York: William Morrow, 1985.

Brooke, John H. "Visions of Perfectibility" in *Journal of Evolution and Technology* 14, No. 2 (2005).

Brown, Terry. *Gene Cloning and DNA Analysis—An Introduction.* London: Wiley-Blackwell, 2010.

Burland, C.A. *The Arts of the Alchemists.* London: Weidenfield and Nicholson, 1967.

Burr, Harold S. *Blueprint for Immortality—The Electric Patterns of Life.* London: Neville Spearman, 1972.

Burr, Michael. *The Man Who Was Frankenstein.* New York: Harcourt, 1973.

Butler, Marilyn. "Frankenstein and Radical Science" in *Frankenstein: Norton Critical Editions.* New York: W.W. Norton & Co., 1995.

Churton, Tobias. *The Golden Builders: Alchemists, Rosicrucians and the First Freemasons.* New York: Weisner Books, 2005.

Cremo, Michael A., and R.L. Thompson. *Forbidden Archaeology: The Hidden History of the Human Race.* Bhaktivdeenta Book Trust, 1993.

Dennis, Rabbi G. *Encyclopaedia of Jewish Myth, Magic and Mysticism.* St. Paul, Minn.: Llewellyn, 2007.

Dodds, E.W. *Echoes of the Gods.* London: Dent, 1918.

Florescu, Radu. *In Search of Frankenstein.* London: New English Library, 1977.

French, Peter J. *John Dee: The World of an Elizabethan Magus.* New York: Routledge and Kegan Paul, 1972.

Fritze R.H. *Invented Knowledge.* London: Reaktion Books, 2009.

Godwin, J., and Robert Fludd. *Hermetic Philosopher and Surveyor of Two Worlds.* New York: Thames & Hudson 1979.

Goldmann, Saul. *Jewish Folklore and Fiction.* London: Erlbaum, 1957.

Gordon, Peter. *Lost Technologies.* New York: Headland Press, 1971.

Hancock, Graham. *Underworld: The Mysterious Origins of Civilisation.* Pittsburgh, Penn.: Three Rivers Press, 2003.

Harris, Sam. *The End of Folk Religion, Terror and the Future of Reason.* New York: Norton, 2004.

Kolisko, Lily. *Workings of the Stars in Earthly Substances*. Privately printed, 1928.

Levy, Steven. *Artificial Life*. New York: Vintage Books, 1992.

McTaggart, Lynn. *The Field: The Quest for the Secret Force of the Universe*. New York: HarperCollins, 2003.

Morrison, Ryan. *Ancient Marvels*. London: Huntingdon Press, 1991.

Rollins, B.A. *The Frankenstein Syndrome: Ethical and Social Issues in the Genetic Engineering of Animals*. Cambridge, Mass.: Cambridge University Press, 1995.

Said, Edward. *Orientalism*. New York: Random House, 1978.

Saxon, A.H. *P.T. Barnum: The Legend and the Man*. New York: Columbia University Press, 1989.

Shaw, Debra B. *Women, Science and Fiction—The Frankenstein Inheritance*. London: Palgrave McMillan, 2000.

Shelley, Mary. Marilyn Butler, ed. *Frankenstein or Modern Prometheus: The 1818 Text*. OUP, 2008.

Singer, I.B. *The Golem*. London: Farrar, Straus & Giroux,1983.

Smith, R.H. *Curiosities*. McDonald Printing, 1899.

Strickland, D.H. "Monsters and Christian Enemies." *History Today*, February 2000.

Thomas, J. *Mechanical Devices in the Ancient World*. London: Fox Publishing, 1969.

Tiptree, Sir James. *Some Notes on Certain Jewish Superstitions*. London: Privately printed, 1852.

Trachtenberg, J. *Jewish Magic and Superstition*. Pittsburgh, Penn.: University of Pennsylvania Press, 2004.

Waschsmuch, G. *The Etheric Forces in Cosmos, Earth and Man*. London: Anthroposophic Publishing Co., 1932.

Bibliography

Webb, James. *The Occult Enlightenment*. London: Richard Drew, 1981.

Wessel, E. *Golem: Story of a Legend*. London: Granite Impex, 1983.

Wilson, C. *Monstrous Imaginings*. New York: Dean & Sons, 1921.

Young, K. *Foundations of Modern Science*. New York: Hamilton, 1932.

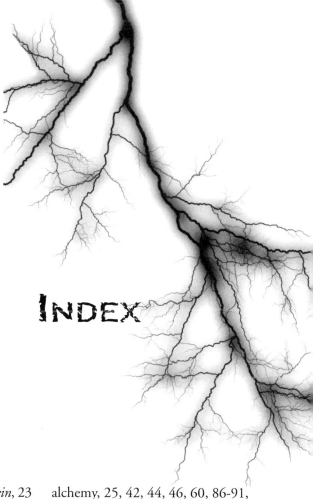

INDEX

Index

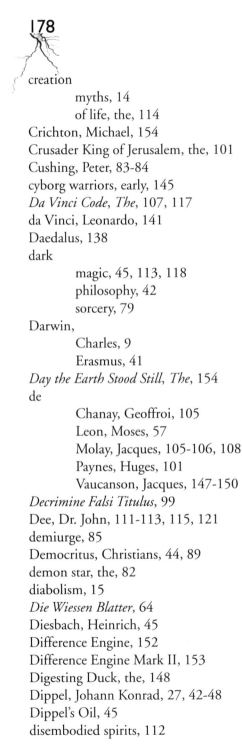

Index

Index

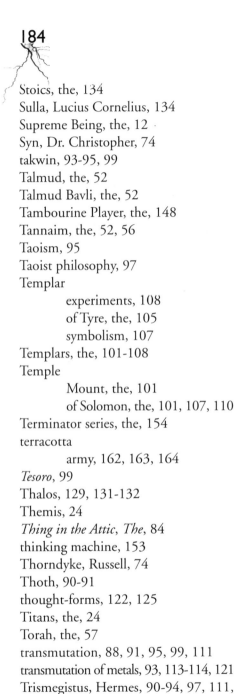

About the Author

Dr. Bob Curran was born in a remote area of County Down, Northern Ireland. The area in which he grew up was rich in folklore—especially the folklore of the supernatural—and this gave him an ear for and an interest in the tales and beliefs of many people. He worked a number of jobs before going to university, where he received a doctorate in child psychology. Even so, his interest in folklore and folk culture was still very much in the fore, and this prompted him to write a number of books on the subject, including *Celtic Lord and Legend*; *Vampires*; *Werewolves*; *Zombies*; and *Lost Lands, Forgotten Realms*. Having taken a degree in history, he now lectures and broadcasts on matters of historical interest, and acts as advisor to a number of influential cultural bodies in Northern Ireland. Most recently he has been working on advisory bodies regarding cultural links between Northern Ireland and the West of Scotland. He currently lives in Northern Ireland with his wife and young family.

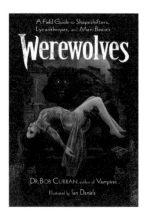
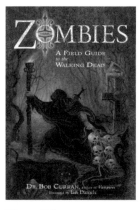

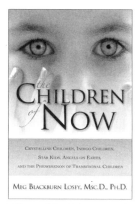
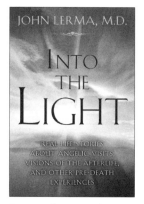